THE LAST FRONTIER

A short history of Alaska

Also by Ben Adams:

ALASKA: The Big Land

HAWAII: The Aloha State

THE LAST FRONTIER

A short history of Alaska

by **BEN ADAMS**

with illustrations by
GEORGE AHGUPUK

New York **HILL** *and* **WANG**

CONTENTS

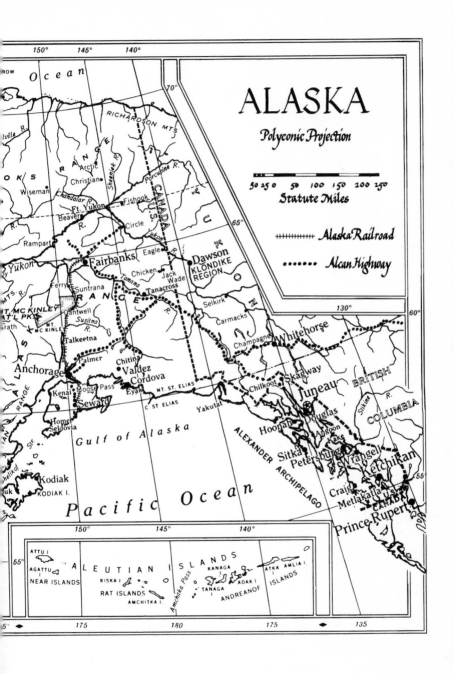

ALASKA

Polyconic Projection

50 25 0   50   100   150   200 250
Statute Miles

++++++++ *Alaska Railroad*

• • • • • • *Alcan Highway*

GEORGE AHGUPUK, the Eskimo artist who illustrated *The Last Frontier,* is entirely self-taught. Born in 1911 in the lonely, windswept village of Shishmaref in northwestern Alaska, within sight of Siberia, he now lives with his wife and four children in Anchorage.

When George was nineteen, he drove his dog team the more than 200 miles to Nome, to visit the only dentist in northwestern Alaska. On the return trip, hunting ptarmigan for his supper, he lost his footing and fell onto broken rocks, injuring one leg.

There was no doctor or nurse in Shishmaref, so his injury bothered him for four years, until he was persuaded to visit the Alaska Native Service Hospital at Kotzebue. An operation and six months in a cast made him a new man.

But his hospital stay did more than mend his leg. He began sketching, at first with a rough pencil on toilet tissue. A nurse bought paper and crayons and encouraged him to make Christmas cards for her. He made a dozen, for which she paid him $2 — his first earnings from his drawings. He left the hospital with a veritable fortune of $10 in his parka.

At home once more, George had no paper, so he experimented with reindeer hide and sealskin. He devised a process of curing the skins which has added much to his unique art style. Every skin must have about eight hours of careful scraping, and then bleaching and drying for about a month, before it is ready to draw on. There are now so many orders for pictures that he uses about 200 skins a year.

Fellow artist Rockwell Kent visited Alaska in the late 1930s and on his return told many people in the States about the Alaskan artist's great talent. Ahgupuk was invited to join the American Artists Group and a number of his drawings have been reproduced as Christmas cards.

In 1951 the commissioners of the Alaska Housing Authority asked Ahgupuk to prepare the story and pictures for their annual report. He accepted, with one limitation: "You must give me free hand," he said. "I do pictures through my eyes. Sometimes maybe Eskimo sees different from white man." He smiled. "Your eyes are big and round. Ours have different shape."

It is particularly appropriate that the first history of Alaska written for young people should have been illustrated by a native Eskimo artist.

THE LAST FRONTIER

A short history of Alaska

1

THE LAND AND THE PEOPLE

WHEN the United States judge for the third district of Alaska set out on his first case, he loaded up his Indian-made basket-style sled. Among the blankets, socks, and food for men and dogs he put a copy of the newly adopted Alaska Code and, as he later recalled, "blank court records for establishing law and order in the wilderness."

Judge James Wickersham had to travel 500 miles in the dead of winter in Alaska's interior from one little gold-mining camp to another to rule on a dispute between two prospectors over mine claims. Wickersham did not complain about the long, difficult trip. It was part of his job.

He started on a beautiful, bright, very cold morning in 1900. The first day out he fell and sprained his ankle when the sled turned over on broken ice. He wore a blister on his good foot trying to favor the other, but he opened the blister and filled it with coal oil. He went on, standing long hours behind his dogsled, although the thermometer fell to thirty degrees below zero the first day and kept going down. Judge Wickersham survived that trip and many others like it to lead the fight for self-government and eventual statehood for Alaska.

Ahqupuk

To hold court the judge had to travel by dogsled or, sometimes, by slow river steamer down the Yukon. When he first got to the little town of Eagle, where he was stationed, he built his own house of logs and made furniture for himself and his family. Then he built a log-cabin court house, the only one for hundreds of miles in the great Yukon Valley. When he wanted meat for the winter, he shot four fat caribou and had them butchered into steaks, roasts, and chops. He put the cuts of meat for a few hours in a tent; the thirty-below weather froze them so hard they rattled like boards.

Life was hard in those gold-rush days in Alaska for the men who had come seeking gold — or freedom or solitude or greater opportunity. It was hard for gold miners and trappers and for United States judges. They had to be brave and daring and adventurous. They had to be resourceful and do things for themselves.

These men were individualists who often had to do without the company of other humans for weeks or months. Yet they were thoughtful of their fellow men and cooperated with one another. "We found a latch string hung on the outside of every prospector's door," Wickersham wrote of one of his trips by dogsled. "It was the custom for any traveler to pull the string which raised the inside wooden bar, walk in, make a fire, and make himself at home." The prospectors always arranged shavings and wood ready for a fire in their iron Yukon stoves, and left a box of matches in sight so that travelers coming in from the cold and wet could warm themselves quickly.

They were pioneers in those days in Alaska, men who not only searched for gold but who also opened up a new country in the face of enormous hardship and dreamed of a future when Alaska's wide open spaces would be occupied by great, prosperous cities and a happy, thriving population.

A great many things have changed in Alaska since Judge Wickersham started out in his dogsled more than sixty years ago; many of the dreams of those days have come true. Alaska's citizens, among them judges, travel these days in the planes that fly everywhere in the new state. There are still some trappers and prospectors who live and work in isolation, but most Alaskans now live in or close to cities. They have radio, TV, daily newspapers, modern elevator buildings, up-to-date community services.

Today Alaska's young people go to school exactly as they would elsewhere, and the educational system is considered one of the best in the nation. Teachers are well paid. Alaskans do not stint their schools. They are justly

proud of their state university. The University of Alaska, founded in 1915 near Fairbanks, is a growing institution now with about a thousand students.

Those who think of Alaska solely in terms of grizzled old sourdoughs and prospectors will be surprised to learn of the new state's vigorous cultural life. There are excellent little theaters with enthusiastic amateur companies in Anchorage and Fairbanks. Concerts are almost always well attended. Anchorage boasts a fine public library, a symphony orchestra, and a community chorus. Many highly regarded artists and writers live and work in Alaska.

Alaska has an active and varied religious life. There are still a number of Russian Orthodox churches, part of Alaska's heritage from its long Russian period. Roman Catholics are the largest single religious group in Alaska, followed closely by the Presbyterians, the oldest of the local Protestant denominations, which sent its first missionaries to Alaska in the 1870s. Many other beliefs are also represented.

Most Alaskans cannot be distinguished from other Americans in dress or appearance. Despite a widespread impression to the contrary, the population is not made up exclusively of Eskimos: there are only about 16,000 Eskimos in Alaska. The Eskimos are one of the three formerly primitive peoples native to the area; the others are the Indians and the Aleuts. All three native groups together make up only a small part of the population today.

While Alaska's native peoples have been rapidly enter-

ing the twentieth century, there are still survivals of an older way of life. In the more remote native villages there are striking contrasts between old and new. Umiaks, traditional open hunting boats, are still used — but they are now equipped with outboard motors. The young people are rock-and-roll enthusiasts — but the men still hunt and fish, and the women still slaughter the whale and the seal as they did in the past.

In fact, Alaska as a whole is marked by striking contrasts. Even in important cities that have modern schools and TV stations there are still unpaved streets. In the bustling metropolis of Fairbanks you can occasionally see a ramshackle log cabin next to spanking-new hotels and apartment houses. Alaska is becoming modernized and industrialized. But it still has a long way to go.

Ahgupuk

Alaska is like the rest of the United States in many ways, but it also has many distinctive features of its own. One difference is the higher cost of living — generally about 50 per cent higher than elsewhere in the United States. This is because Alaska has traditionally had to pay high freight rates for imported goods and because it has lacked adequate transportation and manufacturing facilities of its own.

Alaskans, even city-dwellers, are closer to nature and the outdoors than most other Americans. They love their mountains and rivers. Fishing and hunting can always be done nearby, and these are favorite sports; they are also antidotes to high prices. Many Alaskans keep freezers well stocked with salmon and moose meat.

Perhaps the greatest difference between Alaska and other parts of the United States is in the spirit of its people.

Throughout Alaska is an atmosphere of activity and bustle and enterprise which makes a visit there invigorating. Most Alaskans have all kinds of ideas and schemes, plans for civic improvements or new businesses, proposals of all kinds for building up their state. Alaska attracts people with vision and determination.

A Nebraska farm boy, assigned to Alaska by the Army in 1946, saw the rolling plains around Fairbanks and announced to his buddies that he was going to start a ranch in Alaska. It took him ten years and many heartaches. But he made it, and he and his family now operate a cattle ranch southwest of Fairbanks.

A commercial pilot, who first saw Alaska during World War II, got a glimmer of the tourist possibilities of Alaska's north. He reasoned that thousands of Americans would like to see Alaska's underdeveloped areas with their remote Indian and Eskimo villages. His hunch worked out. His little tourist agency, begun in a tiny office, has grown into a million-dollar business.

Alaska's people are younger on the average than in the rest of the country. And along with the youth of its population come drive, determination, and a spirit of adventure.

Alaska's unique features stem largely from the fact that in many ways it is still a frontier, that its people are modern pioneers building up an underdeveloped, underpopulated area.

Alaska's population has grown rapidly, particularly since World War II, but it still has too few people for so vast an area. It is, of course, by far the biggest of the states. Yet its total 1961 population of about 226,000 is smaller than that of Akron, Tucson, Oakland, or other medium-sized American cities.

Alaska has just begun to make use of the natural wealth

in its rivers and mountains and forests — a total wealth greater than that of any other state. Because the gold rush is so firmly implanted in national history and legend, most people tend to think that gold is Alaska's greatest — perhaps its only — resource. Actually, the value of Alaska's annual salmon catch has for decades been greater than the worth of its gold production. Alaska has many minerals which offer great promise for its future — vast untapped deposits of copper, coal, and iron as well as nickel, tin, uranium, and tungsten. Alaska's almost endless forests, long a wasted resource, are a great potential source of wealth. Perhaps most important of all, Alaska has millions of acres of black gold — petroleum — still waiting to be exploited.

Why is this so? Why does Alaska still need building up and developing? Why does it still need pioneers?

People outside Alaska generally answer the question by pointing to the state's climate and geography. They have been saying for many years that Alaska is too forbidding and cold and barren to sustain a large population and a modern civilization. But the facts do not bear this out.

Alaska does have areas that are arctic and frozen; these have been dramatized in novels, movies, and on television. It also has areas that are mild and temperate. Only about one fourth of Alaska lies in the Arctic or North Frigid Zone. Most of Alaska is habitable by man. Most of it is no colder than the Scandinavian countries, which are today flourishing centers of industry and a highly developed civilization.

Alaska is far too big to be uniform, anyway. There are several Alaskas, in terms of both weather and geography.

The climate of southeast Alaska is so mild that the hardy Alaska sourdoughs refer to it as the *banana belt*. Its winters are no colder than Maryland's; its summers are pleasant but rainy and remind visitors of Portland, Oregon. Southeast Alaska is the part of Alaska closest to the rest of the United States, a relatively short hop by plane from Seattle, and borders British Columbia. A spectacularly beautiful area with fiords, glaciers, mountains, and great forests, it is made up of a necklace of hundreds of islands and a narrow strip of coast known as the Panhandle. Important cities here include Juneau, the capital, and Ketchikan; factories and mills are now beginning to process the region's forest products.

Western Alaska, the vast coastal area extending west of the Panhandle, is certainly habitable. Anchorage, Alaska's newest, biggest, and most modern city, is in this area. Here too is the Matanuska Valley, Alaska's major agricultural area, where huge cabbages and other vegetables are grown and excellent dairy products produced from the milk of local cows. Summers are warm but not extreme in western Alaska; winters are similar to those in North Dakota and Minnesota — cold but far from unbearable.

The extreme western tip of the mainland is the Alaska Peninsula, a great salmon-fishing center. Extending out from this peninsula are the Aleutian Islands, where the Russians first came in their quest for furs. Although their climate is usually temperate, these grassy, almost treeless islands are often fogbound, swept by winds, and subject to violent storms.

Most Americans form their impression of the new state from dramatic movies and novels about central Alaska or the interior. This is the old gold-mining country famed in story and legend. Here is the heart of Alaska, sprawling from the Canadian border to the Bering Sea between the great Alaska and Brooks mountain ranges. It is drained by the mighty Yukon River and its tributaries. Here are seeming-

Ahgupuk

ly endless forests, grassy plains — and the sudden, awesome elevation of Mount McKinley, at 20,320 feet the tallest mountain in North America. Fairbanks, Alaska's second largest city, is the metropolis of the interior. The only other city in central Alaska, far to the west on the Bering Sea, is Nome, no longer as important as it was during the goldrush days but still the home of gallant pioneers planning adventurously for the future of Alaska.

Summers are hot in the interior, and the winter weather is very cold. The thermometer has been known to dip as low as sixty-six degrees below zero in Fairbanks. Old-timers love the cold, dry winters of the interior and the feel of powdery, frozen snow beneath their feet. People can and do live happily in the interior, and point out the fact that

Siberia, which is at least equally cold, is rapidly being industrialized. Alaska's interior has rich potential for future development.

The real wilderness area — perhaps the only one which may defy modernization at least for a long time — is Alaska's arctic, which lies north of the Yukon. Here are the state's green, grassy tundras, rolling prairies where the ground is always frozen under a few feet of topsoil. Wildflowers in surprising profusion color the arctic prairies in summer. Many explorers and nature-lovers prefer arctic Alaska to any other part of this vast state. Despite the extreme cold, they believe man can learn to live here.

Alaska's weather and geography do not explain adequately why it is only now beginning to come into its own. To understand fully why Alaska is still a frontier you must know something of its dramatic and often tragic history. Geography and climate have a part in the story. So do the rivalries of the great nations of Europe and their dreams of empire.

Man has played his role, too — a decisive role. All kinds of men are part of the story: Russians, Englishmen, Americans, even Frenchmen and Spaniards. There were explorers, hunters, traders, politicians, prospectors, speculators, businessmen. There were men who did not understand Alaska and, knowingly or not, held it back; men who grasped the importance of Alaska a hundred years ago; men who had a vision of the potential of this huge area and gave themselves to make it come true.

Alaska was the last corner of the North American continent to be discovered by Western man. The American Revolution had already been fought when the first permanent settlement was made in Alaska. Our forty-ninth state got off to a late start.

Alaska was not settled by England, France, or Spain, the

European powers that figured mainly in the early history of the Western Hemisphere. It was discovered and settled by Russia. This was due in large part to Alaska's geographic position as a peninsula jutting out from the northwestern corner of North America toward Asia. At the Bering Strait it is only fifty miles from Siberia. But Russia was itself until fairly recently a backward country, and it contributed virtually nothing to Alaska's development.

One of the first men who understood Alaska's real importance was a farsighted American — William H. Seward, Abraham Lincoln's Secretary of State. Most people laughed at Seward when he arranged the purchase of Alaska. They did not take seriously his statements that Alaska had great natural resources and was ideally situated to give the United States a bridge to Asia.

For a long time Alaska fared little better under the United States than it had under the rule of Russia. It was neglected and ignored. Its inhabitants received few of the benefits of American citizenship, and the region was a victim of cruel discrimination.

The gold rush suddenly put Alaska in the limelight, and tens of thousands of Americans hurried there by every available boat. Sourdoughs tramped its trails and prospected its streams, proving to the world that Alaska was indeed a treasure-house of mineral wealth.

Not until World War II did most Americans begin to understand that Alaska was not only rich in natural resources but was also a centrally located area both in war and peace. The airplane ended forever Alaska's isolation and made it in fact a bridge between America and Asia as well as between Europe and Asia.

Now Alaska is at last a state in the Union, beginning to grow and prosper, planning to develop its resources for the benefit of the nation and the world. But for almost a century before statehood there were Alaskans who braved every danger and hardship to conquer a great new land, our last frontier.

Alaskans today are carrying on that tradition. They face the future with confidence. They are certain that Alaska will flourish and that its tremendous possibilities for recreation, sightseeing, and industry will soon be utilized by the entire nation.

The story of Alaska is a story of pioneers surmounting natural and man-made obstacles. It is a story that has in it tragedy and comedy, success and failure, greed and self-sacrifice, and — above all — perseverance and heroism. This is a story which should be known to all Americans — because Alaska is a part of the United States and because the future of our country is bound up with the future of this rich, beautiful, challenging forty-ninth state.

2

INTO THE UNKNOWN

WHEN you look at a map of Alaska, you may be surprised by the number of Russian names, like *Baranof* Island in the southeast (on which the town of Sitka is situated) or the Eskimo village of *Shishmaref* on the Bering Sea or *Shelikof* Strait between Kodiak Island and the Alaska Peninsula. When you visit the 49th state you will probably meet people of Russian ancestry with Russian names; you will certainly see here and there old wooden churches with onion-shaped domes, in which worship is still the traditional Greek Orthodox service of the Russians. These are all reminders of the Russian portion of Alaska's history, of the period when Russian explorers discovered Alaska, when the native peoples of Alaska were subdued by Russian conquerors, and when Alaska was part of the Russian Empire.

It all started at the end of the seventeenth century with Peter the Great, the restless, ambitious Czar who made great changes in old Russia. Peter invited some of the great scientists of Europe to come to his new capital, St. Petersburg, and work for his government. He admired their keen minds and shared their endless curiosity. He was particu-

larly interested in the little-known eastern domain of his
own empire in Siberia and what lay beyond.

During Peter's reign Russians pushed relentlessly to the
east. Cossack hunters and fur traders had for generations
been making their way through the Siberian wilderness;
they finally reached Kamchatka on the Pacific in 1697.
They sent a delegation to see Peter, bringing him gifts of
rich furs and telling him the rumors they had heard from
the natives about land far to the east and to the north.
Shortly afterward Peter visited England, Holland, and
France, where he talked with geographers at the great uni-
versities and with sailors and explorers. From them he
heard of the long quest for a short cut to the wealth of
China and India, for a Northwest Passage by water from
Europe to Asia. Peter felt that perhaps a solution to the
mystery lay within his reach. He recalled the talk of the
Siberian merchants and he speculated whether Siberia was
joined to America, where the other European powers were
then busily carving out empires. He wondered whether he
might not claim a great domain for Russia in the new world.

For years Peter was diverted from his dream of expansion by the long and costly war between his country and
Sweden. But in 1719 he sent two Russian explorers on a
secret voyage off the Siberian coast. Their findings proved
little. Then, in 1724, shortly before his death, he instructed
Vitus Bering, a Danish-born officer in his navy, to build a
vessel at Kamchatka and sail "along the coast which ex-
tends to the north and which (since we do not know where
it ends) seems to be a part of America."

"With this in view," the Czar further instructed Bering,
"you are to try to find where it is joined to America, and
to reach some settlement in European possession, and to
inquire what it is called, and to make a note of it, and

secure exact information and to mark this on a map and then to return home."

For the next seventeen years, while five different rulers sat on the throne of Russia, Bering tried to carry out his orders. When he started, the northwestern coast of North America was a mystery which had been explored for only about a hundred miles north of San Francisco's Golden Gate. By the end of that time he had answered the old question of whether Asia and America were joined together and had blazed a trail for other navigators into the whole North Pacific area.

Bering's task sounded easy — on paper. But even before he could start his voyage he had to get to the Kamchatka Peninsula with men and supplies for building ships. This entailed a journey of more than 5000 miles across mountains and steppes, rivers and swamps, and across a great inland sea. Then he had to venture into unknown waters toward unknown territory.

In the summer of 1728 Bering sailed through the narrow strait between Siberia and North America that now bears his name. He sighted and named St. Lawrence Island, which is now part of Alaska, and Big Diomede, which is owned by Russia. Fog prevented him from seeing nearby Little Diomede Island, which today belongs to the United States. Bering's voyage accomplished its main purpose. He proved that Asia and America are separate continents, not joined as Peter had thought.

The learned geographers at the Academy of Science in St. Petersburg refused to believe his report. They had maps of their own (which they had constructed from the tales of sailors and from their own imagination). They decided that Bering could not possibly have been where he said he had been or seen what he said he had seen. Bering was ridiculed and jeered in the Russian capital.

After many delays and long discouragement, he finally got approval for a second expedition. But this time Bering was saddled by the Russian government with an elaborate order which contained enough instructions to keep scores of explorers busy for several generations. Among other things, he was supposed to chart the entire coast of Siberia as well as the American coast north of Mexico, visit Japan, and open mail service by land from Russia to the Chinese border. Only with the help of an influential friend was Bering able to eliminate an order from the Russian Admiralty that he reach Alaska by way of Africa.

For several years Bering faithfully followed his instructions, explored the Siberian coast, and charted its waters.

In 1741 he launched his final expedition in two small ships. One, the *St. Peter,* he commanded himself; the other, the *St. Paul,* was under the command of his assistant, Alexei Chirikov. Each ship was manned by seventy-six men, among them several scientists. Bad luck dogged the explorers. They were hit by a heavy storm off the Aleutians and their tiny vessels were separated.

Chirikov and his men first sighted the coast of Alaska, a bare twenty-four hours ahead of Bering. On July 15, 1741, they saw a heavily wooded island, one of the Alexander archipelago in southeast Alaska. After searching in vain for a suitable place to anchor in a sheltered bay, Chirikov sent one of his two boats ashore with ten men to bring back water.

Officers and men waited anxiously for their return. After several days, Chirikov sent four well-armed men in his only remaining boat. Again nobody returned. In the midst of the vigil on the *St. Paul,* the lookout spotted two boats and a great cheer went up from the crew. But these were not the lost sailors in the *St. Paul*'s boats. They were natives in canoes, waving their paddles in what seemed to be hostile gestures. Chirikov reluctantly concluded that his men had been killed and set sail for home.

The return voyage was stormy and difficult. The crew lacked food and water and most of the sailors were weakened by scurvy. They tried to stop at one of the Aleutian Islands to replenish their supplies but were driven off by heavy winds. They suffered from cold and from the icy spray that swept the deck. Chirikov himself was tormented by tuberculosis. Finally the little vessel made it back to Avancha Bay in Kamchatka.

In the meantime, Bering's *St. Peter* sailed eastward for several weeks without sighting land. Discouraged by his apparent failure, Bering changed course and sailed north

through heavy fog. On July 16 the fog suddenly lifted —
and there stretched before the weary, storm-battered crew
the rugged coast of Alaska, dominated by a great snow-
capped mountain. Since it was St. Elias Day, Bering named
the peak in honor of the saint.

Bering had carried out the most important part of his
mission. He had discovered America by sailing east. He
had proved again that Siberia and the North American
continent are separated by water. Now he was anxious to
return home as soon as possible.

The *St. Peter* anchored off Kayak Island and a party
headed by Georg Wilhelm Steller, a German-born botanist,
landed. Steller wanted time to study the wildlife of the
island, but Bering ordered him back after a few hours.

Bitter anger flared between the two men, who were strik-
ingly different in age and temperament. Steller was young
and impetuous, heedless of danger. Bering was sixty years
old; he was ill, a veteran of many hazardous voyages, and
his natural caution was reinforced by experience.

The quarrel between Bering and Steller has resounded
through the years, and both have probably been treated
unfairly by historians. Steller made important studies (which
were long ignored) of the marine life of the North Pacific,
while Bering was regarded as something of a coward and
his explorations were downgraded. Actually, Bering made
invaluable contributions to man's knowledge of the world
and his charts were so accurate that they served mariners
for many years.

Bering's desire to turn back as soon as possible was
based on sound reasons, not lack of courage. He was wor-
ried about his lack of food, the seaworthiness of the *St.
Peter* in the face of storms, and the tricky waters of the
Alaska coast — still difficult to navigate even with modern
instruments. It is at least debatable, in the light of what

happened, whether any of the crew would have survived to tell the story if Bering had not turned back when he did.

On the long return voyage to Siberia the *St. Peter* was buffeted by storms and deluged with heavy rains. Lacking fresh vegetables, the men grew ill with scurvy. Bering's gums were swollen, his joints stiff. Finally, the *St. Peter* put in at what is now known as Bering Island to find food and cover.

There was little shelter on the cold, windswept island. In the shifting sands the men hollowed out dugouts and covered them with driftwood. They placed Bering in one of these and respectfully tried to brush away the sand blown by the wind over his half-frozen body. But it was too late to save their leader. He died on December 8, 1741.

Many others died — thirty-one in all. The survivors gradually managed to regain their strength on Bering Island. Steller got members of the crew to join him in collecting the green plants that would combat scurvy. Gradually the men became well enough to kill the strange animals they saw in the ocean, and the fresh meat gave them new energy. The *St. Peter* was too battered by storms to be useful, but a new ship was built from its wreckage. The survivors returned, bringing news of their discoveries and souvenirs of their voyage which proved beyond any question where Bering and his men had been.

Even in his few hours on Kayak Island, Steller collected plants then unknown in Europe and Asia as well as implements used by the natives, who fled at the approach of the strangers. He also captured a large bird with bright blue feathers — a blue jay. He recalled having seen a similar bird in an illustrated book by an Englishman on the natural history of the Carolinas and Florida. "This bird," Steller said, "proved to me that we really were in America."

Before his youthful death in Siberia on his way back to Russia, Steller managed to complete a scholarly work on the unknown animals he had discovered on Bering Island: the sea cow, the sea lion, the fur seal, and the sea otter. The beautiful furs of the seal and the otter created a sensation in Siberia when they were displayed by members of Bering's crew.

Siberian merchants and traders examined the furs closely, and were excited by the news that Alaska abounded in the creatures that bore them. They soon found that sea-otter fur commanded fabulous prices in Russia, Europe, and China — where it was used to trim the robes of the nobility. Soon the merchants organized parties of Siberian hunters called *promyshlenniki* — boisterous frontiersmen — who sailed off in crude boats for the promised land in Alaska.

Before long Catherine the Great, carrying on Peter's plans for exploration, sponsored several expeditions to Alaska. Other explorers — British, French, Spanish — were soon attracted to Alaska both by the old dream of finding the Northwest Passage and by the hope of wealth from fur-bearing animals. Alaska was no longer an unknown land, a blank on all the maps. Bering's voyages had opened the North Pacific for trade, conquest, and settlement.

3

THE FIRST ALASKANS

THE Russians were far more interested in the fur-bearing animals of Alaska than in the people who lived there, but they realized from the start that Alaska was inhabited by primitive peoples. They assumed that some of Chirikov's men had been killed by hostile natives, and Steller had brought back with him tools and implements he found on Kayak Island.

Who were the people found by the Russians? Where did they come from? It was believed until fairly recently that they had been there from time immemorial and had developed independently their own languages and handicrafts. Even now there is much about the origins of Alaska's native peoples that is not clear to us. But it is known that they came originally from Asia. It is likely that they followed much the route from Siberia that the first explorers did.

Thousands of years before Bering and Steller, daring Oriental hunters from northeast Asia reached the shores of the Pacific. They came in an endless search for food, for a place to live less crowded by other people competing for game and fish. Perhaps on a clear day they looked out and saw land, then pushed onward to explore in crude boats. They might have seen one of the Aleutians and gone island-hopping toward Alaska in slow stages. Or perhaps they crossed by land at some remote time when Asia and America were joined at the place now called Bering Strait.

Whether they traveled by water or land or both, the first inhabitants came to Alaska from Asia. They pushed south along the coast, settling in what is now the United States; others went still farther, into Central and South America. Probably only after the warmer lands to the south were fairly well populated did the first permanent settlers begin to live in Alaska in any great number.

For centuries they lived throughout most of Alaska,

hunting and fishing, building homes and boats, developing several distinct cultures of their own. These were primitive peoples, but they carved wonderful designs on ivory and wood and stone; some of them wove beautiful blankets; others made intricate, watertight baskets of grass; they had their own legends and religions. Sometimes they fought each other, but they were relatively peaceful compared with the more highly developed civilizations of Europe and Asia. The technical advances of western Europe were unknown to them — but so were the dread diseases and the use of alcohol introduced later by Europeans.

By the time the first white men arrived, in the eighteenth century, there were four distinct groups of native peoples in Alaska: the Aleuts, who lived on the Alaska Peninsula and the Aleutian Islands that extend far out into the Pacific; the Eskimos, who occupied the shores of the Bering Sea and the Arctic Ocean; the Athapaskan Indians of the interior of Alaska; and the Tlingit and other Indians who lived in the relatively mild climate of southeast Alaska.

The Aleuts were sea people, great hunters of seals, sea lions, even whales in the single or double-hatched skin boats they called baidarki. As they paddled they sometimes looked in awe at the mainland and called it *Al-ay-eksa* —

Ahgupuk

the great land. In Aleut it is spelled Alaxsxaq. That is how Alaska got its name. They were completely at home on the water. A Russian observer who saw them long ago in their primitive state said that there was "something majestic" in the appearance of an Aleut in his baidarki but that he appeared clumsy and ill at ease on dry land.

The Aleuts drew their sustenance from the sea, not from their treeless islands overgrown with grass and soft moss. Their food consisted largely of the flesh of sea animals, shellfish, fish, and sea birds. Their boats were made of the skins of seals and other creatures of the sea. They also made their clothes of skins. Men and women wore shirt-like garments very much like the parkas of the Eskimos but without hoods.

Several families of Aleuts, sometimes as many as 150 people, lived together in big houses as much as 240 feet long and 40 feet wide. These houses were sunk into the ground and covered with dry grass and sod. The walls and roof supports were made of driftwood or whalebone.

The women wove and sewed with great skill, using needles made of the bones of fish or seagulls and making thread from sinew. Their greatest achievement was making baskets from beach grass, which they split with their long fingernails and then wove. These baskets were practical because they held water and food without leaking; they were also lovely to look at, covered with brightly colored designs and symbols.

To the north of the Aleuts lived the Eskimos. It seems strange to us that primitive people, without modern implements and conveniences, should settle on the shores of the Arctic Ocean. Yet the Eskimos and their predecessors not only did so but also managed to produce a remarkable civilization there. During the 1940s a University of Alaska expedition found the remains of an ancient city at Point Hope, well north of the Arctic Circle. Homes were laid out along streets; ivory carvings found there were carefully and beautifully executed. All signs pointed to a culture

about 2000 years old, more advanced than that observed in relatively recent times among the Eskimos.

The implements found at Point Hope were similar to those produced at the same time in northern China and in parts of Siberia, helping to prove the Asian origin of Alaska's native peoples. The Eskimos, who followed the prehistoric people whose remains are found at Point Hope, adapted themselves so well to arctic weather and terrain that Europeans and Americans who have tried to live in the far North have had to learn from them.

Because life was always a struggle, the Eskimos had to join together in small groups of families and share with each other both the good and the bad. The hunter usually divided with other families the seals and caribou he killed. Whales and large animals were the common property of the group. To work hard so that all could survive was the great unbreakable rule of the Eskimos. No one was allowed to be idle; any man who didn't use his traps or his fish spear or his boat had to allow others to use them to better advantage.

Like the Aleuts — and in the face of even greater difficulties — the Eskimos wrested their living from the sea. From seal or walrus skins they made seaworthy one-passenger canoes, called kayaks, and larger boats to carry several men and supplies, called umiaks. In these frail boats, using only a harpoon as a weapon, they hunted regularly for whale as well as seal and walrus.

From the animals they killed the Eskimos made everything they needed. The sea provided both food and clothing. The Eskimos considered seal liver a special delicacy. Another treat was muktuk, a piece of whaleskin with some blubber still attached. The Eskimo diet was fatty, an essential in the subzero temperature.

They used seal blubber for fuel, and it gave a good flame

for both cooking and light. They used the scraped seal hide for the soles of their fur boots or mukluks. Their warm parkas, made of caribou skin, had a fur ruff to protect the face.

There was fun as well as hard work among the Eskimos. Every year at the end of the whaling season, usually in June, a big festival was held. It was called *Nelukataktut,* after the blanket-tossing game traditionally played on this occasion. A good player would remain upright on the walrus hide no matter how many times he was bounced up, but a poor one might break his back.

On long winter nights the Eskimos gathered in their community house and danced to the rhythms of flat skin drums. Or they sat and told tales of brave hunters and myths out of the past. One story was about an old woman who ruled over all the animals in the sea but who had a bad temper and was easily irritated. When she was angry, she stirred up the waters, causing big waves and sudden storms.

The Eskimos also liked to tell how the stars came into being. Once, the story goes, there were two moons, Father Moon and Mother Moon. Father Moon grew tired of traveling from east to west all the time, as he had been instructed by the Little Man of the Tundras who ruled the heavens. He decided to take a trip to the southern horizon instead. The Little Man of the Tundras became very angry. He picked Father Moon up in his mighty hands, crushed him into little bits, and blew the pieces off into the sky. That is how the stars were born. That is also why Mother Moon wanders alone from east to west.

The heaven of the Eskimos was not in the cold, dreary sky but in the warm earth. When a man died, he went down to the world far below the frozen tundra where it was always comfortable. For a while his spirit hovered about looking for a place to rest. But when a child was born, the dead man's name was given to the newborn and the spirit could rest.

Usually the Eskimos pampered their children. One ex-

planation was that this was out of respect for the departed whose spirit lived in the child. In any case, children were never punished and rarely scolded. Nevertheless, to the first European observers they did not seem spoiled and obeyed their parents as well as western children.

The Athapaskan Indians who have long lived in Alaska's vast interior are a tall, handsome people related to the Navajos, Apaches, and Hupais far to the south. Originally the Athapaskans lived in Canada, but were driven north by warlike tribes about eight hundred years ago. They settled in the spectacularly beautiful mountain-rimmed valleys of the interior.

When the moose and the caribou were plentiful in the forests and there were many salmon and other fish in the streams, the Athapaskans thrived. But when hunting and fishing were poor, they often died of hunger. They suffered much during the long, cold winters. In the legends of the Athapaskans there are many stories of starvation, and there are also some which indicate that early members of the tribe were at times reduced to cannibalism.

The Athapaskans were a nomadic people. They did not try to cultivate the soil or establish permanent settlements. They wandered through the rivers and forests, following

game. They dried the salmon, their favorite fish. They roasted the caribou and used its skin for clothing. With simple tools they carved the wooden canoes in which they traveled along the rivers.

More advanced were the Indians of southern Alaska — who had also migrated from Canada, but more recently than the Athapaskans. They lived in a milder climate, and since food was more plentiful they established permanent settlements. The land was not suitable for agriculture, but game and fish were never lacking. There were no starvation legends among the southeastern tribes, the Tlingits, the Haidas, and the Tsimpshians.

The Tlingits, by far the most numerous and important of the three, lived in large community houses, fifty to a hundred persons in a house and perhaps a dozen houses in a village. The houses were solidly constructed and held up by posts made from the trunks of great trees. The different families in each house lived on a raised platform along the walls. In the center the ground was bare; here was the central fire for the whole house.

Throughout southeast Alaska and even in Canada, the Tlingits were feared as fierce warriors. In battle they wore carved wooden helmets, and over their faces were ferocious masks representing the killer whale or the mammoth bear. They sailed the rivers and bays in high-powered war canoes big enough to hold dozens of men. They often enslaved the people they conquered in their frequent wars and sometimes the slaves were offered as religious sacrifices by the Tlingit chiefs.

The Tlingits were animists — they believed there were spirits in all things, including the objects around them. They gave friendly greeting to the glaciers and trees and mountains. When there was thunder in the sky, they said that the Thunder Bird was flapping his wings. The lightning flashed from the Thunder Bird's eyes when he hunted whales. On his back was a huge lake which spilled over on the earth when he flapped his wings. The earth rested on a great post — not unlike the posts that held up Tlingit houses. The world was guarded by Old Woman Underneath, who used to get restless every once in a while and shake things up; when she moved, there were earthquakes.

Animals, on whom they were so dependent for food and clothing, had a special place in the life of the Tlingits. They believed animals had magic powers and were man's ancestors. One of their favorite stories tells how the raven put the sun and the moon and the stars in their place.

Once a chief's daughter had a baby boy with dark, bright eyes like those of a raven. So the grandfather named the

baby *Raven*. One day Raven cried very hard and did not stop until the grandfather gave him a box full of stars to play with. The stars suddenly blew away through the smoke-hole of the house and up into the sky. Then the grandfather gave him a second box, which contained the moon. Raven played with the moon for a while. But the moon bounced through the doorway and then up into the heavens. Finally, the grandfather took the sun out of his third and last box and fastened it to a string around the child's neck. But the boy suddenly changed into a raven and flew up into the sky with the sun in his beak. Then he tossed the sun high into the sky — where it has stayed until this day.

There were two great divisions among the Tlingits. One was called the Ravens, the other the Eagles. These in turn were divided into clans or groups of families. The Raven, Frog, Sea Lion, and Salmon clans were all part of the Raven people. The Wolf, Bear, Eagle, Whale, and Shark clans belonged to the Eagle people.

Each clan had its own totem or emblem based on a figure of its particular bird or animal. Out of these totems grew the remarkable art of the Tlingit and Haida Indians.

Totem poles were great logs carved and painted with figures of ravens, wolves, sharks, or whatever other creature the clan was named for. By the use of totem carvings the clans told the stories of their ancestors. The totem pole was therefore a sort of family tree. The house posts of the community houses had similar decorations. Totem designs formed the central part of the chilkat blankets, woven from yellow cedar and wool by one group of Tlingit Indians. Totem figures were also used to ornament the baskets and stone vessels made by Tlingit women.

Unlike the Aleuts and Eskimos, the Tlingits were a trading people. Their relatively rich life made it possible for them to carry on commerce with other peoples. They traded food and slaves for sharks' teeth and mother of pearl from Indian tribes farther south, and from the Athapaskans they obtained caribou skins and sinew. The chilkat blankets often served as money in their trading.

The primitive peoples of Alaska — the Aleuts, the Eskimos, and the Indians — had made their peace with nature and survived the rigors of the rough and often brutal *promyshlenniki*. The Aleuts were friendly and gracious to the newcomers and taught them the lore of the land and of the animals and fish.

A Russian navigator who visited the Aleuts in 1794 paid them this tribute: "Their behavior is not rude and barbarous, but mild, polite, and hospitable. At the same time, the beauty, proportion and art with which they make their instruments and apparel evince that they by no means deserve to be termed stupid, an epithet so liberally bestowed on those whom Europeans call savages." But hunters from Siberia were contemptuous of the natives and greedy for the fur of the seal and the sea otter.

One of the first groups of *promyshlenniki* landed on Attu in the Aleutian Islands and began to mistreat the native women. When the Aleuts protested, all the males of one settlement were massacred. That was how Massacre Bay — from which the United States launched its operation to recapture Attu from Japan during World War II — got its name.

Increasingly the Aleuts resisted the Russians, and in 1764 they revolted, destroyed three ships, and killed the crews. There was bitter fighting for a couple of years until the Russians finally subdued them. Sometimes the Aleuts have been described as docile and lacking in manhood, but in this instance they fought back as best they could until they were subdued by superior force.

The Aleuts were required to pay tribute of furs and skins to the Russians. Later they were made virtual slaves and forced to go out in hunting parties while most of the Russians stayed behind and caroused. Often the Russians committed acts of sheer brutality. An eyewitness told how, after a skirmish with the Russians, "an elder Aleut and another man were lured to the Russian ship. There they were put on deck and their arms and legs stretched out by thongs, subjected to tortures; scalding hot tar was poured on their bodies. After that the elder was beheaded. . . ."

Not until later did the Russians encounter the Tlingits — who lived up to their reputation as fierce warriors. In fact, the Russians never really subdued them. The Eskimos in the north and the Athapaskans in the interior were less immediately threatened since the Russians never occupied their territory. But eventually all the native peoples paid a heavy price for the civilizing influence of the white man. They suffered from torture and enslavement, but even more from the ravages of disease and alcohol.

From the first coming of the Russians the Aleuts and then the Tlingits fell prey to many diseases, including smallpox, tuberculosis, and measles — a terrible killer among the natives. As whalers stopped at Eskimo villages and hunters pressed on into the interior, the natives there also succumbed to these and other diseases.

Gradually the Alaskans' food supply was threatened. In only a few years the Russians slaughtered so many seals and sea otters that it became harder and harder for the Aleuts to live in the old way. In addition, liquor and the lure of trinkets hopelessly undermined the established way of native life.

It was a long time until the native peoples of Alaska began to enjoy some of civilization's benefits.

4

DREAMS OF EMPIRE

LATE in the eighteenth century, while Siberian merchants, frontiersmen, and hunters were following up Bering's discoveries by organizing expeditions to the Aleutians for seals and sea otters, a boy named Alexander Baranof was growing up in the town of Kargopol in the cold north of Russia. Born in 1747, Baranof became Russia's man of destiny and empire-builder in Alaska. He had just the right temperament and training for what was at best a difficult job.

From his earliest days he was used to cold weather and felt at home in the thick dark forests surrounding his home town. Alexander was shorter and thinner than his playmates in Kargopol, but he was tough and wiry, a born outdoorsman. Even as a child he was an expert shot. He learned how to dry and stretch skins and sent them off to Moscow to earn a little extra money for his none-too-wealthy family. But Kargopol was a dull place for an adventurous boy, a provincial backwater untouched by all the new ideas from western Europe which were then exciting young people in Moscow and St. Petersburg.

When he was fifteen, Baranof ran away to Moscow, where he worked for some years as a clerk for a German firm. Moscow in the 1760s had many foreign businessmen, merchants, and bankers. Alexander learned German, acquired a modest education on his own, and got something of an idea of the great world that lay beyond Russia.

Then he returned to Kargopol, where he went into business for himself. He was still restless; he had the spirit of a pioneer. Siberia far to the east appealed to many young Russians then in much the way the West of the United States was for generations to draw enterprising young Americans, so to Siberia Baranof went at the age of thirty-three.

There he became a successful manufacturer, producing glass by a new process which attracted attention even in faraway Moscow and St. Petersburg. But he was not content merely to make glass. Baranof went to the far north of Siberia, where he traded with the Chukchi, a primitive people very much like the Aleuts and Eskimos he was later to meet in Alaska.

A chance meeting on one of these northern trips changed Baranof's life. He became acquainted with Gregory Shelikof, a rich merchant and fur trader who had been to Alaska and in 1784 had founded on Kodiak Island the first Russian colony in the new world. Shelikov was looking for someone to go to Kodiak and bring order into his company's operations there. He needed a man who was rugged and hard-boiled, who could control the Siberian hunters he had sent to Alaska. These *promyshlenniki* were rowdy men, many of whom had been picked up in the taverns of Siberian towns and shanghaied aboard ship or persuaded to sign long-term contracts while hopelessly drunk. Now they were getting out of hand in Alaska, ruthlessly killing off the natives, spreading infectious disease, and spending much of their time drinking vodka.

To Shelikof, Baranof seemed the man who could tame

the *promyshlenniki* and make his Alaskan fur operation pay off. At first Baranof was reluctant to go. Then he had a stroke of bad luck: a shipment of furs he had bought in the North was stolen, and he was deeply in debt. He decided to go to Alaska to try to retrieve his fortune.

So at forty-three, Baranof set sail for the Alaskan wilderness on Shelikof's little high-pooped vessel, the *Three Saints*. But the ship was wrecked in the Aleutians, and Baranof had to get to Kodiak in an open native boat. It was a stormy voyage — but by no means as stormy as the situation he headed into in Alaska.

Everything seemed to go against Baranof at first. Life was hard in the crude, tiny Russian settlement at Kodiak. He had trouble with the *promyshlenniki* — who were naturally restless, particularly during the long winters when they were shut up most of the time in their log cabins. Several times they plotted to kill him. He had trouble with the Tlingit Indians, who repeatedly rebelled. He also had trouble with some of the colonists Shelikof had sent him, Russian serfs unsuited to the primitive frontier life of Alaska.

In addition, Shelikof turned out to be a difficult man to deal with, always nursing some grievance or other against Baranof. One of his complaints was that Baranof was too friendly with British and Yankee sea captains who came on trading or exploring expeditions to Alaska. In addition to facing problems inside his own company and competition from abroad, Baranof also faced active rivalry from other Russian firms. His men even had armed clashes with *promyshlenniki* from one of these firms.

But Baranof was tough and persistent, the leader the Russians needed in Alaska. He could drink as hard as any of his men, and he joined them in wild Russian dances during the cold winter nights. But he subdued their revolts and managed to get work out of them. Washington Irving described Baranof as "a rough, rugged, hard-drinking old Russian; somewhat of a soldier; somewhat of a trader; above all a boon companion of the old roystering school, with a strong cross of the bear."

Baranof refused to be beaten down by adversity. He organized large parties of Aleuts, virtually enslaving them in the process, to hunt the sea otter up and down the Alaska coast and as far away as California. He expanded Russia's hunting operation and opened trade with British, American, and Spanish interests. When the Russian government decided in 1799 to merge the rival companies in the Alaska fur business, Baranof was the logical man to head the new Russian-American Company which was given a government monopoly in Alaska. He became the company's general manager and the Czar's governor in the American colony.

Baranof insistently spurred the building of ships for his colony. Through the years he constructed fourteen vessels despite a lack of tools and equipment. This tiny fleet made it possible for him to trade all over the Pacific, to send his ships to Japan, Hawaii, and California.

Baranof grudgingly permitted Russian Orthodox priests to convert natives and found schools. But he had little enthusiasm for these missions. He was interested in furs, not souls.

After his hunters killed off the fur-bearing animals of the Aleutians, he transferred his operations to southeast Alaska and established a fort at what is now called Sitka on Baranof Island.

There was always danger in the Alaskan wilderness, and in 1802 the fierce Tlingits stormed and captured the fort at Sitka. Baranof complained that they wore several coats of wooden armor "wherefore neither bullets nor arrows nor

pikes were powerful enough to defeat them." The Russians also said resentfully that the Tlingits had guns supplied by rival British and Yankee traders.

About this time Baranof was made a nobleman by the Czar as a reward for his services in Alaska. Sadly he wrote the directors of the Russian-American Company, "I am now a nobleman, but Sitka is destroyed. I cannot live under the burden, so I am going forth either to restore the possessions of my august benefactor or to die in the attempt."

Baranof was wounded in the attack on the Tlingits, but not too seriously. The Russians recaptured their fort, and the town of Sitka was established nearby. Baranof established his capital at Sitka, and a gay little city it soon became. Sailors and adventurers came there from all over the world. There were parties, and frequent balls at which Russian officers in full-dress uniform danced with ladies in splendid evening gowns. A trader who did business for a while with Baranof wrote to the American merchant John Jacob Astor, "They all drink an astonishing quantity, Governor Baranof not excepted. I assure you it is no small tax on the health of a person trying to do business with him."

From Sitka Baranof continued to send ever greater shipments of furs to Siberia and to build up the Czar's domain. Actually, Baranof's scope went beyond the confines of Russia's colonies scattered along the Aleutians and southeast Alaska. In the early years of the nineteenth century, officials in Moscow and St. Petersburg began spinning heady dreams about a great Russian empire in the North Pacific which would rival those of the great powers of Europe.

Alaska was to be the northern anchor of this empire, but there was also a plan for establishing colonies farther south along the coast of California, which was only lightly held by the Spaniards. The Russians also cast their gaze across the Pacific toward the Sandwich Islands, as the Hawaiian Islands were then called. As governor of Alaska, Baranof was expected to translate these dreams into fact.

Shortly after Sitka was rebuilt in 1804, there arrived at the Russian capital of Alaska a handsome and elegant Russian nobleman, Nikolai Petrovich Rezánov, who brought Baranof word of the grandiose schemes being hatched in Russia. Rezánov was himself one of the eager expansionists in the Czar's government. In fact, he had been largely responsible for the idea of setting up the Russian-American Fur Company under official sponsorship as a means of blocking the aspirations of other European powers in Alaska.

Rezánov's mission from Czar Alexander I was to establish trade with Japan, strengthen the Russian position in the Pacific, and supervise Baranof's operations in Alaska. Rezánov was both a dreamer and a man of action. He arrived at Sitka shortly after it was recaptured from the Tlingit Indians. There were no adequate quarters for the distinguished visitor and his party. Sanitary conditions were conspicuous by their absence. The whole little town stank of uncured fur and rotting fish. Most important, there wasn't enough food. Rezánov moved promptly. He bought supplies from the *Juno,* a visiting American ship. Then he purchased the ship itself and sailed for the California coast, hoping to trade Alaska furs for food.

But the Spaniards were suspicious. The *Juno* sailed through the Golden Gate under the muzzles of Spanish guns. When Rezánov arrived at the Presidio, the Spanish fort at San Francisco, he was given all the honors due him as ambassador of the Czar. Governor Arillaga of California rode up from Monterey to meet him. The Spanish officials had been forbidden to trade with the Russians, however, and Rezánov's eloquence failed to persuade them.

Then love found a way. Rezánov fell in love with Doña Concepción Arguëllo, sister of the Spanish commandant of the Presidio, and she with him. They announced that they would be married. Her parents stormed. The governor was displeased. But the couple were firm. In the end, the parents gave their permission, if approval could be won from the Pope in Rome. So Rezánov won the hand of the beautiful fifteen-year-old Concepción. He also broke down the governor's resistance to trade and succeeded in selling his shipload of furs to the Spaniards in return for the food he needed for the Russians in Alaska.

Rezánov unloaded the precious food he brought to Sitka and then left for St. Petersburg to obtain the Czar's sanction for trade with Spain and his marriage to Doña Concepción. But he never reached the Russian capital. He died of fever and exhaustion while hurrying back across Siberia. Concepción mourned for her betrothed, and then foreswore love. She entered a convent and lived there in seclusion until her death many years later.

Did Rezánov truly love Concepción, as legend has had it in California for more than 150 years? Or was Rezánov pretending love for diplomatic reasons because an alliance with a high-placed Spanish family would help the imperial plans of the Russians? This very unromantic explanation was the one he offered in a letter to Czar Alexander, but perhaps he was only trying to win the Czar's approval for the marriage by pointing out its advantages to Russia.

In any case, the dream of Russian empire did not die with Nikolai Rezánov. Baranof soon started seeding the northern California coast with markers that read *Land belonging to Russia*. In 1812 he established a colony at Fort Ross, about fifty miles above San Francisco.

Baranof also pursued the Russian plan for establishing a beachhead in Hawaii. For some time he maintained friendly relations with King Kamehameha of Hawaii. Russian naval officers stopped off there, looking over the situation with a view to establishing colonies.

In 1815 Baranof dispatched to Hawaii a German adventurer, Dr. Georg Anton Scheffer, a ship's doctor and former surgeon for the Russian police. Posing as a botanist, Scheffer ingratiated himself for a time with Kamehameha. When he helped the king recover from a cold, Kamehameha rewarded him with a gift of land in what is now downtown Honolulu. Scheffer promptly started building a fort there and aroused the suspicions of Yankee traders in Honolulu. They feared that Scheffer was plotting to take over the Hawaiian Islands and deprive them of their profitable sandalwood trade. At their insistence Kamehameha ordered the fort abandoned.

Protected by three Russian ships, Scheffer moved his operations to the island of Kauai, where King Kaumualii was plotting against Kamehameha. Scheffer hoped to take advantage of this rivalry to become master of the islands. But Kamehameha cracked down and ordered his expulsion. The king of Kauai yielded, and that ended the Russian dream of taking over the Hawaiian Islands.

The Russian government disowned Scheffer and rebuked Baranof for wasting money on the unhappy adventure. This was one of the incidents that led to Baranof's downfall. In 1818 he was replaced as governor after almost thirty years of service to the Czar in Alaska; he was seventy-two then. It was a hard blow, somewhat softened by the fact that the new governor married Baranof's daughter Irina. Baranof died on his way back to Russia, little appreciated for his efforts to hew an empire out of the wilderness.

Perhaps the most important Russian in Alaska after Baranof was Father Innokenti Veniaminov, a Greek Orthodox priest who, starting in 1823, set up a number of missions and schools. Veniaminov for the first time won the respect and affection of the Aleutian islanders, who had been alienated by the harsh and inflexible ways of earlier Russian missionaries. He was a serious student of Alaska's native peoples and he made major contributions both to their education and to our knowledge of their cultures.

In other respects things went steadily downhill for the Russians after Baranof's death. Their colony in California was not looked on kindly by Mexico after that country won its independence from Spain. Both Britain and the United States also resented Russian expansion in the New World. The Monroe Doctrine of 1823 was aimed in good part at Russia. Although the Russians hung on for many years to their foothold at Fort Ross, they eventually sold their land and buildings to Captain John Sutter — shortly before the discovery of gold on Sutter's farm started the gold rush to California. In Alaska the Russians were confronted with growing British competition. The British Hudson's Bay Company engaged in trading and hunting in territory claimed by the Russians. There were clashes between agents of the two countries and a brush between Russian and British warships.

Alaska became a problem for the Russians. It was difficult to hold against the British — and it hardly seemed worth the trouble. Increasingly Alaska dried up as a source of income for the Russian-American Company; for many years it was actually a liability.

By the 1850s it was becoming clear to the Russians that they had made a mess of things in Alaska. They had showed neither the ability nor the vision to use the area's great natural wealth. They had killed off the seals and the sea otters, wasting millions of skins in dyeing. They had burned millions of others to keep world prices up. They failed to engage in farming or to explore the interior and to exploit Alaska's vast mineral resources. They brought disaster to the Aleuts and the Indians, infecting them with new diseases and depleting the supply of animals for food and clothing. The contributions of Father Veniaminov and other missionaries had to be measured against the suffering brought the native peoples. The Russians had little to show for a century of exploration and colonization in Alaska. The bright hopes of Baranof and Rezánov for empire in the new world had withered.

5

SEWARD'S FOLLY

SECRETARY of State William H. Seward was relaxing at home in Washington, D.C., on the night of March 29, 1867, playing a quiet game of whist in the parlor with his family, when the Imperial Russian Minister, Baron Edouard de Stoeckl, was unexpectedly announced.

Seward and Stoeckl had been negotiating secretly for some time about the purchase of Alaska by the United States. Stoeckl was anxious to sell — to unload the liability Alaska had become for Russia. Seward was even more anxious to buy — to push the American frontier farther westward to the Pacific.

There had been little haggling over price. Stoeckl was authorized to sell for as little as $5 million; at one point he even considered *giving* Alaska to the United States. But for bargaining purposes he asked $7 million. Seward promptly agreed. He even added $200,000 to pay for various hunting concessions that had been leased by the Russians. That was how the price of $7.2 million was arrived at. Now the Russian diplomat was bringing word that his government had approved the deal.

"I have a dispatch, Mr. Seward, from my government

by cable," Stoeckl said excitedly. "The Emperor gives his consent to the cession. Tomorrow, if you like, I will come to the department, and we can enter upon the treaty."

"Why wait till tomorrow, Mr. Stoeckl?" Seward said, pushing away the card table. "Let us make the treaty tonight."

The Secretary of State and the Russian Minister hurried to the Department of State. Seward hastily summoned Senator Charles Sumner, chairman of the Senate Foreign Relations Committee. A few other aides on both sides were sent for, and the lights burned late that night as the small group ironed out the details for the purchase of Alaska. The treaty was signed at 4 A.M. on March 30. Later that day President Andrew Johnson sent a terse special message to the Senate submitting "a treaty for the cession of Russian America."

Pandemonium broke out in Washington — and throughout the country. Few people had heard of Alaska. Editors and members of Congress rushed to their atlases and encyclopedias to look up this unknown wilderness that had been acquired by the Secretary of State. What they read there, written largely by geographers and other alleged experts who didn't know too much about Alaska either, failed to inspire enthusiasm.

Seward was condemned and abused. *Seward's Folly* has become the best known of the epithets used at the time. Others were *Johnson's Polar Bear Garden, Walrussia, Polaria,* and *Icebergia.* One Congressman, unencumbered by any knowledge of the subject, declared that "every foot of the soil of Alaska is frozen from five to six feet in depth." The New York *Tribune* commented bitterly, "We may make a treaty with Russia but we cannot make a treaty with the North Wind or the Snow King." The New York *Herald* ran a fictitious ad mocking the purchase:

CASH! CASH! CASH! Cash paid for cast-off territory. Best price given for old colonies, North or South.
Any impoverished monarchs retiring from the colonization business may find a good purchaser by address-
ing W. H. S., Post Office, Washington, D.C.

This ad was fairly representative of public sentiment.
Those people who knew anything at all about Alaska knew
that the Russians were getting rid of their American colony
because they had not made a go of it. What they could not
understand was why Seward was so anxious to buy that in
less than twenty-four hours he concluded the negotiation
of a treaty and had it sent to the Senate for ratification.

A few Americans, who turned out to be right, predicted
that Seward would be longer and more favorably remembered for his purchase of Alaska than for his many other
contributions to the United States, including his stalwart
opposition to slavery and his service as Lincoln's wartime
Secretary of State. These optimists included the people who
had been to Alaska and who knew something about it.

There were American fishermen and whalers, familiar
with the wealth of Alaska's waters, who knew that the purchase would be profitable to the United States. In fact, they
had been at that very time bombarding Seward with re-
quests to negotiate with Russia for fishing rights off Alaska's
shores — little realizing that Seward was planning to buy
the whole place for them.

There were also strong supporters of Seward among the
scientists, explorers, writers, and other members of the recently abandoned Western Union expedition to Alaska.
The object of the expedition, launched when several attempts to lay a telegraph cable across the Atlantic failed,
was to work on one phase of an alternate route westward
through Washington Territory, British Columbia, Alaska,

under the Bering Sea, across Siberia, and thence to the capitals of Europe and Asia. The project was dropped in 1867 after the transatlantic cable was successfully laid.

The members of the expedition had returned with some solid knowledge about Alaska's geography and resources, plus a conviction that it was by no means destined to remain an uninhabited wilderness. One important member of the expedition, William Henry Dall, was a scientist. He patiently gathered all the facts he could and in 1870 published his findings in *Alaska and Its Resources,* the first American book about our new territory.

Seward was acquainted with some of the firsthand reports about Alaska. He knew that it abounded in untapped natural wealth. What motivated him even more strongly, however, was his profound belief that America's destiny lay in the Pacific. Seward was driven by a desire to expand the boundaries of the United States, which was recovering rapidly from the carnage of the Civil War and beginning its swift rise as one of the world's great powers. He was eager to take over a number of Caribbean islands. But he was, above all, interested in westward expansion. He described the Aleutian Islands as "stepping stones across the Pacific Ocean" and Alaska as a bridge between America and Asia.

Senator Sumner, one of the great orators of his time, told the Senate that Alaska would strengthen America's Pacific defenses and provide a link with the people of Japan and China. His most persuasive argument, however, was that failure to ratify the treaty would weaken the traditional friendship between Russia and the United States. This argument finally nudged a reluctant Senate to approve the purchase — with only one vote more than the necessary two-thirds majority. What saved Alaska for the United States was the overwhelming tide of good feeling for Russia which prevailed throughout the North and West at that time. Members of Congress were willing to waste a few million dollars to do Russia a good turn.

Earlier in the century there had been some tension between the two countries. The United States had been alarmed by Russian expansion in the Western Hemisphere, but the wheel of international politics later took a sharp turn and threw the two nations together in warm friendship.

Russia was Great Britain's enemy in a bitter rivalry for territory and empire, climaxed by the Crimean War in 1854–56. United States relations with Britain were also strained, and there were some sharp clashes over the boundary line between Oregon Territory and British Columbia. In self-interest, Russia and the United States drew closer.

During the American Civil War both Britain and France were friendly to the Confederacy. Only Russia refused even to receive a Confederate ambassador and gave diplomatic support to the Union cause. Czar Alexander II freed the Russian serfs about the same time Lincoln freed American Negro slaves. When units of the Russian navy put into New York and San Francisco in 1863, the country greeted them with enthusiasm. The public assumed this was a show of strength for the Union. Actually, the Russians had headed for United States ports because they feared that their ships would be destroyed in another war with Britain. But everywhere Russian naval officers were received with toasts "to Lincoln the Emancipator and Alexander the Liberator." Secretary of the Navy Gideon Welles said feelingly, "God bless the Russians." A few years later Oliver Wendell Holmes wrote:

> Throbbing and warm are the hearts that remember
> Who was our friend when the world was our foe.

One reason Russia was anxious to complete the deal with Seward was her belief that Alaska would be taken by the British or the Americans anyway; of the two she preferred the United States to have it. When the Russians discovered there was gold in Alaska, this made them all the more eager to sell to the United States. They were convinced that American prospectors would soon be swarming over Alaska, as they had earlier over California. Selling to the United States, they reasoned, would cement the friendship between the two countries and avoid possible future friction over Alaska.

Despite the warm national feeling for Russia which was Seward's ace in the hole, the Secretary of State's troubles were far from over. After the Senate ratified the treaty of purchase, the House had to put up the money, and the Representatives balked. A memorandum found later among President Johnson's papers said that the Russian ambassador had handed out substantial sums to influential members of Congress to ease their doubts. But opposition persisted. The House rang with oratory. One Missouri congressman declared that "the acquisition of this inhospitable and barren waste would never add a dollar to the wealth of our country or furnish any homes to our people."

It took more than a year for the House to provide the necessary $7.2 million, and in the end Seward forced the issue. Nine months before the House acted, he had formally taken over Alaska for the United States and confronted Congress with an accomplished fact. The American flag had been raised over Sitka. "Shall that flag which waves so proudly there now be taken down?" asked an Indiana congressman. "Palsied be the hand that would dare to remove it. Our flag is there, and there it will remain." The House had no alternative to agreeing.

Visitors to Sitka can still see a few rusted cannon with

the Russian imperial crest; they stand on a little ridge over-looking dark-green wooded islands set like jade in the sparkling blue channels and inlets of the Pacific. A few feet away is a flagpole with a barely legible inscription on a brass plaque at its base: "On this site Oct. 18, 1867 the American flag was raised on the territory of Alaska by members of Company E 9th Infantry United States Army."

Here the century-old Russian dream of empire in the Americas finally ended in a formal ceremony. Russian and American troops stood stiffly at attention while a commissioner of the Czar's government announced that Alaska was being ceded to the United States. Guns boomed from Russian and American warships. The last Russian governor of Alaska, Prince Matsoutkoff, gave the signal for the Russian double-eagle flag to be lowered and for the Stars and Stripes to go up. Legend has it that the Russian flag got caught in the ropes and would not come down. A man was then sent aloft to tear it down, and he threw it to the wet earth. The Princess, watching from her window, wept for the passing of the old.

A reporter, writing for a San Francisco newspaper, exulted, "The Russian eagle has now given place to the American and the national colors floated over a new widespread territory. Our dominion now borders on a new ocean and almost touches the old continent — Asia. Democratic institutions now extend over an area hitherto the possession of a despotic government. The occasion inspired the soul of every American present, and as the officers retired three mighty cheers were given and we all rejoiced that we now stood on American soil."

There were few enough cheers back home. Eventually a reluctant House approved the purchase and an indifferent people received the news that our country had acquired a vast new territory. Alaska was off to a bad start; many years passed before it won genuine national acceptance and became part of the United States in fact as well as name.

6

UNCLE SAM'S STEPCHILD

As soon as the American flag was raised over Sitka, settlers began pouring into Baranof's old capital. A California congressman, arguing for the purchase of Alaska, had said that when Americans "get hold of a country there is something about them which quickens, vitalizes and energizes." Life did quicken in Sitka — for a while.

Frontiersmen, businessmen, restless pioneers like those who peopled the Old West all came to the little Russian city. They found the climate milder than they expected, rainy at times, but usually pleasant and bracing, rarely too cold for comfort. They liked what they saw — a vista of green-forested islands in a maze of sparkling Pacific inlets against a backdrop of snow-covered mountains.

Living off the land was no problem. There were deer in the woods and plenty of salmon and other fish in the streams. There was plenty of fine timber for building homes.

Settlers began to claim land and put up homes and stores. Mingling with the Americans were several hundred Russians, employees of the Russian-American Company gathered from all over Alaska to wind up its affairs. They were told that they had three years to make a choice either to go back to Russia or to stay in Alaska and enjoy all the privileges and rights of American citizenship. Many were tempted by the prospect of remaining.

Sitka became something of a boom town. Stores, saloons, and businesses were started — even two bowling alleys. Before long there was a newspaper, the Sitka *Times*. There were great plans afoot to develop the area, to exploit its resources, to set up a local government.

But a little oversight in Washington sent all the optimistic plans awry. Congress did belatedly and reluctantly grant President Johnson's request for the appropriation to purchase Alaska, but it brushed aside his request that a government be set up for the new area. Congress took no such action for seventeen years. In fact, it did nothing at all about Alaska, and by doing nothing Congress made it impossible for Uncle Sam's vast northern territory to prosper and flourish.

Alaska was given no government, no schools, no law-enforcement machinery. There was no provision for homesteading, mining, or lumbering. The settlers who flocked to Sitka wanted to set up a city government. They were told that it was illegal either to put aside the land for a townsite or to elect an administration. Congress had provided no authority for local self-government.

The settlers wanted to claim land for homes. In all the new territories acquired by the United States since the early days of the republic, pioneers had simply taken a piece of land and built a log cabin there, secure in their legally recognized squatters' rights. This first-come, first-served principle had ruled in the West and made it possible for newcomers to cultivate the land and acquire property. Later, homestead laws made it possible for farmers to get up to 640 acres in the West at little or no cost. But the newcomers to Alaska were told that all this was illegal.

A week after the American flag was raised over Sitka, the Department of the Interior discovered that there was an 1807 law which prohibited settlement of land acquired by treaty unless specific provision had been made by Congress. Since Congress had made no such provision for Alaska, the government announced that military force could be used "to remove the intruders."

The hopeful pioneers who had arrived in Sitka to make their fortunes in the new land got the bad news soon enough. Many of them naturally grew discouraged and drifted back home. Most of the Russians also left in disgust. The promise of American citizenship seemed to mean little in Alaska.

Senator Ernest Gruening, a former territorial governor of Alaska, summed up the story of those early years with this comment:

> During that period in Alaska no hopeful settler could acquire a title to land; no pioneer could clear a bit of the forested wilderness and count on the fruits of his toil, or build a log cabin with the assurance that it was his; no prospector could stake a mining claim with security for his enterprise; property could not be deeded or transferred; no will was valid; marriage could not be celebrated; no injured party could secure redress for grievances except through his own acts; crime could not be punished.

Kipling put it even more succinctly: "There's never a law of God or man runs north of Fifty-three."

Simply by default, the military for a time provided Alaska with what little government it had. Some five-hundred soldiers under General Jefferson C. Davis came to Alaska to take over the new acquisition from the Russians.

Because there was nobody else to do the job, the Army was in charge — but it lacked both the authority and the experience to run Alaska.

The soldiers were restless in the wilderness. They manufactured whiskey from the molasses they imported in large quantities, drank too much, got into fights with the Indians, and generally provided the native population a poor introduction to their new rulers. Far from introducing law and order, they were a major cause of lawlessness.

After ten years the soldiers were withdrawn to put down the Nez Perce uprising in Idaho. Customs Service personnel were then left as the only representatives of the federal government in Alaska. Alaska didn't yet enjoy the status of a territory, but Congress made it a customs district —

so a customs collector was for a time the highest (and only) federal official in Alaska.

The withdrawal of the soldiers heightened fears of an Indian uprising that would wipe out Sitka. The frantic citizens asked repeatedly but in vain for a United States warship to protect them. A British naval vessel came north from Vancouver Island and remained until an American warship finally arrived. For the next five years Alaska was ruled, again by default, by the naval commanders who happened to be stationed at Sitka.

Except for greater chaos, things seemed little changed from the days of the Russians, when the Russian-American Company was in charge of Alaska. After Seward's purchase, an American firm took over all the assets of the Russian monopoly. It, too, enjoyed a monopoly — by act of Congress.

Before completely forgetting about Alaska, Congress passed in 1870 "An Act to prevent the extermination of the fur-bearing animals of Alaska." A closer reading showed that the law simply leased exclusive seal-hunting privileges on the Pribilof Islands to a group of businessmen in San Francisco who formed the Alaska Commercial Company. The effect was the exact opposite of that stated in the title of the law.

The Alaska Commercial Company's fur trade was immensely profitable, and the money it paid the government for its lease of the sea islands alone compensated the government for the purchase price of Alaska in about twenty years. But the already depleted sea otters were exterminated and the seals were slaughtered so wantonly that they were soon in danger of extinction. The walruses were slaughtered just as ruthlessly: in the 1870s alone, about 100,000 were killed by commercial hunters.

Much the same thing happened with the salmon. About

this time someone discovered that this delectable fish could be canned and sent to the United States for sale. Soon canneries, financed by Seattle interests, were springing up everywhere. Fishermen built barricades across the streams and killed the salmon wholesale.

The new fishing industry did little to help build up the economy. Since Congress had provided no system of taxation, for many years the canneries paid no taxes at all. They brought in Chinese workers and other cheap labor, with the result that virtually no employment was provided for the local population. Thus there early began a pattern whereby Alaska's wealth was extracted by outside interests without benefit to the area and its people.

Even more serious than the destruction of natural resources was the injury to Alaska's native population. For the Aleutian islanders the seal had been the main source of life. Now they had to kill the seals for the white men — but in return received few of the blessings of civilization. No schools were built for them in those early years. Their housing and living conditions were poor, their food supply increasingly scanty. The toll from new diseases mounted. The Eskimos to the north were threatened with starvation by the onslaught against the seal, walrus, and whale on which they had depended for centuries for food and shelter.

Nor did United States rule open up new opportunity for the daring and pioneering Americans who flocked to Alaska after Seward's purchase. Alaska was off to a poor beginning under the American flag. It paid heavily for national ignorance, indifference, and even hostility. Alaska was described as Uncle Sam's stepchild — which it surely was, for too long a time.

7

THE SOURDOUGHS

THE Russians knew there was gold in Alaska. So did the American members of the Western Union expedition to Alaska: they had seen nuggets displayed as trinkets by friendly Indians. The trouble was that nobody had ever found very much of it. But nobody had ever really looked.

The rumor of gold was enough to draw prospectors from the American West and from Canada. They started drifting into Alaska soon after Seward's purchase. They panned in the creeks and rivers of southeast Alaska and in the tributaries of the mighty Yukon, deep in the interior. For years they failed to find a strike rich enough to make it worth while to take the gold out. But they kept on trying.

The gold prospectors were rugged men who dared to explore an unknown wilderness and who knew how to live on the land with only a gun and a pack they could carry on their backs. These were the sourdoughs, the old-timers who won their nickname from the pancakes they made without yeast from a dough they fermented from flour and water.

The sourdoughs were individualists. Many were eccentrics, men who wanted to get away from trains and cities

and sought not only gold in Alaska but the peace of its wild spaces. There were learned men among them who could recite Greek and Latin poetry, Ph.D.s from Oxford and from the great colleges of the United States like Harvard and Yale.

There were grizzled veterans — like Ed Schieffelin, who had discovered a mountain of silver in Arizona and founded the town of Tombstone where Wyatt Earp shot it out with the Clantons. Schieffelin had made a fortune in Arizona. But he pressed on in Alaska, searching tirelessly and unsuccessfully for gold.

There was a famous trio of partners — Arthur Harper, a man with a big beard and the square face of a biblical prophet who had been prospecting in Canada and Alaska for almost half a century; Al Mayo, a wiry former circus clown; and LeRoy Napoleon McQuesten, a big man with bold mustaches who had been an Indian fighter in the West. The three became traders, joining forces in establishing posts along the Yukon and thus financing their quest for gold.

McQuesten was known best for two things — his open-handed bounty to any prospector needing grub or equipment and the remarkable thermometer he kept in his store. This device consisted of four bottles: mercury, whiskey, kerosene, and Perry Davis' Painkiller. If the mercury froze, it was only about forty degrees below zero. If the whiskey froze, it was plenty cold — and colder still when the kerosene froze. But when the painkiller froze it was −70° and time to stick by the fire.

Although most sourdoughs wanted to be left alone, they also believed in cooperation. They knew they had to help each other if they were going to survive in the bitter cold of the interior. When they formed their own organization, the Yukon Order of Pioneers, its motto was *Do unto others as you would be done by*. And the crusty, hard-boiled prospectors lived up to it. Every man's cabin was a refuge for every other against the snow and ice of the Yukon trails.

There was comradeship and honesty among the sour-doughs, and they blamed the later rise of crime on the cheechakos — tenderfeet — who thronged to Alaska at the height of the gold rush. In one of his novels about Alaska, Rex Beach put it this way:

> There weren't any crimes in this country till the tenderfeet arrived. We didn't know what a thief was. If you came to a cabin you walked in without knocking. The owner filled up the coffee-pot and sliced into the bacon; then when he'd started your meal, he shook

hands and asked your name. . . . If there was no one
at home, you took what you needed.

When there were enough prospectors in any area, they
established their own primitive frontier democracy. There
was no effective government in Alaska; the miners had to
set up their own. They made their own laws at miners'
meetings, established their own crude criminal code —
punishing murder with hanging and lesser crimes with ban-
ishment, whipping, or fines.

It wasn't until 1880 that the sourdoughs made a really
rich strike. Two prospectors, Joseph Juneau and Richard
Harris, were exploring along the creeks and mountains to
the Gastineau Channel, one of the innumerable salt-water
inlets of Alaska's inside passage where gold was usually
found when they struck pay dirt. The word quickly spread
to prospectors throughout Alaska who had been searching
in vain.

A rude frontier town with saloons, stores, and hotels
sprang up in the area. There was a big dispute about the
name of the new town. Both Juneau and Harris wanted the
honor. Juneau finally won out and the future capital of
Alaska was named after this early prospector, but the dis-

trict around Juneau was named Harrisburg after Harris.

The sourdoughs had for some time been protesting Washington's total neglect of Alaska. Now they started holding miners' meetings in Juneau, passing resolutions and demanding that the people of Alaska be given some kind of government and some measure of democracy and representation. The discovery of gold made it hard to brush aside their petitions completely. Seward's Folly turned out to be too valuable to ignore. In 1884, seventeen years after Seward bought Alaska, Congress passed a law setting up a government for Alaska.

The law of 1884 didn't give the prospectors everything they wanted, by a long shot. But it represented progress. Unlike the western states, Alaska was not declared a territory, the usual preliminary to statehood. It was given the lesser status of a district. Only about $25,000 a year was provided to govern this huge area of 586,000 square miles and only a handful of men assigned to run it. All of them, from the governor down, were appointed from Washington. While it was denied an elected legislature and representation in Washington, Alaska did make some gains. United States mining laws were applied to Alaska, and it became legal for prospectors to stake claims. At last, $40,000 was appropriated for schools for native and white children.

This belated nod from Congress did not end the clamor for self-government; the demand increased. One of the battlers for equal rights for Alaska was Alfred P. Swineford, a former Michigan editor who was appointed governor in 1885. Swineford fought for education for Alaska, steamship service, better mail service, and the right of Alaskans to elect their own officials.

Governor Swineford claimed that a lobby in Washington was deliberately trying to delude the general public into

"the belief that there is nothing of value in Alaska save its fur-bearing animals." He said that interests which had gotten in on the ground floor feared that self-government might put an end to their monopoly and curb some of their practices. Again and again the governor bitterly protested "unjust withholding from Alaska of political rights never before denied to any section or territory or any fraction of the American people since the adoption of the Federal Constitution."

The setting up of a school system created a great opportunity for Sheldon Jackson, one of Alaska's most devoted friends and important builders. Jackson, a missionary born in upstate New York, made several trips to Alaska in the 1870s and wrote a book about it. He urged the Presbyterians to establish a mission in Alaska; when this was done he was appointed its director. He founded schools and missions — and also urged self-government. In 1886 Jackson was made general agent for Alaska education, at a salary of $1200 a year. Although hampered by lack of adequate transportation, he traveled all over Alaska by dogsled and boat. In little more than a year he started sixteen schools in southeast Alaska and several in western Alaska.

In 1890 Jackson traveled north to the Bering Sea and the Arctic Ocean on a government cutter to open new schools. There he soon discovered that the Eskimos were in serious danger of starvation. He realized that it would not do much good to teach them English or try to save their souls unless they could first be helped to get enough food.

The Eskimo problem grew out of the fact that the walrus and the whale, on which they relied for food and clothing, had been slaughtered almost to extinction. On the same trip Jackson visited the Siberian coast and saw that the natives there were deriving a livelihood from herds of domesticated reindeer. It seemed to him that the Alaska Eskimos could be saved if they were given reindeer.

So Jackson crusaded for a congressional appropriation to purchase reindeer for the Eskimos and import experts who could teach them to raise and use the animals for food and clothing. Turned down by Congress, he wrote letters to newspapers all over the East and raised enough money to buy some reindeer. Finally Congress did make a small appropriation. The reindeer helped to save the Alaska Eskimos and proved their chief sustenance for many years.

Jackson didn't get along too well with the rough-and-ready prospectors who felt that he was too much concerned with the Indians and Eskimos and not enough with the white settlers. But both sourdoughs and missionaries contributed to the building of Alaska.

The discovery of gold by Juneau and Harris brought about, directly and indirectly, many benefits for Alaska. But their strike failed to enrich these two men or most of the other prospectors who flocked to the Juneau area. The gold there was embedded in hard quartz and had to be dug out with picks or blasted out with dynamite. Efficient hard-rock gold mining requires expensive machinery, and eventually two huge, rich mines were established — one in Juneau and the other in Douglas, across the Gastineau Channel. The miners looking for easy-to-get placer gold had to go elsewhere.

Most of them went north to the Yukon, where they searched patiently year after year. Sometimes they made strikes, although not big or spectacular ones. They found gold on the Fortymile River, on Preacher's Creek, the legendary stream where a preacher had once seen gold lying around by the spoonful, and on the other streams that feed the Yukon.

Mining camps and towns sprang up in those areas where gold was found as prospectors flocked there, hoping for the massive strike that would make them all rich. These looked like typical frontier towns. But there was little of the shooting and the lawlessness so prevalent in the Old

West. The miners' meetings usually enforced law and order.
There were saloons and dance halls, but there were also
theaters and books. In the mining town of Circle, far north
on the Yukon, sourdoughs cheered Shakespeare's plays in
the Grand Opera House and established a library filled
with the classics and standard reference works.

The sourdoughs were in the forefront of Alaska's many
fights for self-government. They were bitter at what they
felt was the denial of Alaska's rights, at the stripping of its
resources by outside interests, at the indifference of the
government in Washington. Sam Dunham, a sourdough
poet, expressed their resentment in his "Alaska to Uncle
Sam":

> Sitting on my greatest glacier,
>   with my feet in Bering Sea,
> I am thinking, cold and lonely,
>   of the way you've treated me.
> Three and thirty years of silence!
>   Through ten thousand sleeping nights
> I've been praying for your coming,
>   for the dawn of civil rights.
>
> When you took me, young and trusting,
>   from the growling Russian Bear,
> Loud you swore before the Nation
>   I should have the Eagle's care.
> Never yet has wing of Eagle
>   Cast a shadow on my peaks,
> But I've watched the flight of buzzards,
>   and I've felt their busy beaks.

For all their grumbling and grousing, the sourdoughs
were deeply devoted to Alaska. They came to find their
fortunes in its streams. But they stayed to tame the wilderness and to develop America's last frontier.

8

THE GREAT GOLD RUSH

GEORGE Washington Carmack went to Alaska in search of peace and solitude. Instead he found gold. It was he who unwittingly put Alaska in the headlines and started the mad Klondike gold rush in the closing years of the nineteenth century.

Carmack was a restless man who didn't like crowds and cities. Neither had his father, who crossed the prairies in a covered wagon in the California gold rush of 1849. George was born across the bay from San Francisco, went to Alaska as a young man and stayed there.

Even the bustling little mining camp of Juneau was too crowded for him. He pushed steadily northward into the interior, winding up finally in Canadian Yukon Territory, across the border from Alaska. More at home with Indians than with white men, he married an Indian girl known as Kate, and most of his friends were Indians. Carmack was far from ignorant or illiterate, however. He had an organ and a modest library in his cabin on the Yukon; sometimes he wrote poetry about the solace he found in the quiet forests.

One warm day in 1896 he went fishing at the mouth of

the Klondike River, famous among the Indians for its salmon. With him were his wife and two of her brothers,
Skookum Jim and Tagish Charley. They were catching and
drying salmon when they saw a tall, lean prospector wear-
ing a broad-brimmed miner's hat. This was Robert Henderson, a former sailor and old-time miner who had hunted
for gold all over the world.

Henderson told them that he had found gold at Gold
Bottom Creek.

"What are the chances of locating there?" Carmack
asked. "Everything staked?"

"There's a chance for you, George," Henderson said,
"but I don't want any of those Siwashes staking on that
creek."

Henderson didn't like Indians; he used the contemptuous
term *Siwashes,* a corruption of the French word for savages.

Skookum Jim became angry. He told Carmack that it
wasn't right for the white man to kill the Indian moose and
caribou and take all his gold.

Carmack, brushing this incident aside, said it was a big
country and that they could find a creek of their own.

Jim was more interested in gold than most of his fellow
tribesmen, and he seems to have spurred his. companions
to hunt for Henderson's creek.

They prospected for several days, and had another brush
with Henderson at Gold Bottom Creek. Henderson gibed
at Carmack's Indian friends and told them to go away.
They did — and the results made history.

Jim guided them to Rabbit Creek, later called Bonanza
Creek, where he had prospected before. There they found
a big nugget glittering with gold. It was no freak. When
they panned the gravel, it turned out to be incredibly rich.

On August 17, 1896, the three men staked claims and
set out for the mining camp of Fortymile to register their

claims. On the way Carmack told a number of prospectors about the discovery they had made.

Henderson said later that Carmack promised to notify him if he found anything. Perhaps Carmack was angered at the way Henderson had treated his Indian companions. In any case, he told almost everybody except Henderson.

At first the miners laughed at Carmack when he told them excitedly about his rich claim. He wasn't a real prospector and he was known for his lively imagination. But they stopped laughing when they saw the gold. They knew it was the real thing — the big strike they had sought so long.

From all over the Yukon sourdoughs flocked to the Klondike, deserting Circle and the other nearby mining camps in Alaska. Frantically they grabbed up all the promising claims on Bonanza Creek, many of them later valued at hundreds of thousand of dollars.

Chance, rather than skill or experience, often made the difference between poverty and wealth. At first many of the prospectors didn't realize how rich their claims were and they sometimes sold out for a few hundred dollars. One miner, Russian John Zarnowsky, disposed of his claim for a side of bacon and a sack of flour. Another prospector, late for the best claims, reluctantly staked a small, wedge-shaped fraction of a claim left by the others. He tried to sell it for $900, then tried unsuccessfully to lease it. In the end, he was forced to mine it himself. The claim paid off more than $500,000.

Clarence Berry, a poor California farm laborer who came to Alaska to find gold, was working in Colonel Bill McPhee's saloon in Fortymile when he heard of Carmack's strike. This was his big chance. But he had no money, no food, no dogs. He hoped McPhee would help him.

"Sure, Clarence, here is the key to the cache," McPhee said. "Help yourself."

Berry struck it rich, went back to California to settle down with his wife on a ranch and made another fortune from oil. Years later he heard that McPhee's Washington saloon had burned down. He wired McPhee to rebuild and restock and to draw on him for everything he needed.

Wealth eluded some of the old-timers like Henderson. But for others it came in the nick of time. An Austrian immigrant named Antoine Stander had spent all his funds to come to Alaska and was at the end of his rope. He was too late to get in on Bonanza Creek. But together with four partners he found a creek even richer than Bonanza, called Eldorado Creek. There were small claims on this creek that turned out to be worth a million dollars.

In the fabulous fall and winter of 1896 a crude town called Dawson sprang up at the juncture of the Klondike and Yukon rivers. There were many millionaires and near-millionaires in Dawson. But they lived in tents or rough log cabins, and they didn't have enough to eat. All winter and spring the little mining town hovered near starvation. The Yukon was frozen over and no food could come in from the outside. Nor could the miners leave for the states with their fortunes. Everything was scarce. Prices sky-rocketed.

Many who struck it rich were not as level-headed as Berry. Some, spoiled by wealth, became arrogant and vain. Quite a few gambled away their fortunes. Claims were won and lost on the turn of a card as the miners sweated out the spring of 1897, waiting for the Yukon ice to break and for the riverboats to come and take them to St. Michael's on the Bering Sea, where they could get ships to take them back home.

Finally the great day came, on July 15, 1897, when the first miners from the Yukon, bearded and ragged but carrying suitcases full of gold, shambled off their ship onto San Francisco's Embarcadero. Two days later an even bigger group arrived in Seattle. The Seattle *Post-Intelligencer* carried blazing headlines:

> *GOLD! GOLD! GOLD! GOLD!*
> 68 Rich Men on
>   The Steamer *Portland*
> STACKS OF YELLOW METAL

The whole country went wild. Crowds trailed the prospectors everywhere. The newspapers were full of reports of their doings. And people throughout the country prepared to take off for the Klondike at once.

It is hard today to understand the impact of the Klondike strike unless we grasp something of the background. The news came in the midst of what we have come to call the Gay Nineties and think of as a time of bicycles built for two, barbershop quartettes, and sentimental songs. It was a time when great fortunes were being made in sugar, oil, railroads; a time of great wealth and lavish spending. But the Gay Nineties were not gay for everybody. They were also a time of depression, a time of heartbreak and suffering. And it seemed to many, probably erroneously, that the high price of gold was to blame for their troubles, that times would get better if only gold prices would go down. At just this point the news about the Klondike broke, promising a plentiful supply of gold and lower prices. To millions of Americans the gold of the Klondike appeared to offer a personal way out of unemployment and destitution as well as an answer to the nation's troubles.

The Pacific Northwest, hardest hit by the depression, went craziest over Klondike gold. But all over the country men (and many women) sold businesses, gave up jobs, and prepared to go off to the Yukon. Indeed, the madness spread all over the world, to Australia, Great Britain, Italy, the Scandinavian countries.

All kinds of fantastic schemes were hatched. Klondike Bicycles were supposed to provide a swift and painless journey straight to the gold fields. Yukon Boatsleds were advertised as assuring safe amphibious transportation, as well as a burglarproof compartment for gold. There was even a sure-fire X-ray machine to find gold. Millions of shares of fraudulent stock in nonexistent Yukon mining companies were sold to the public. Many of these schemes were profitable for their promoters if not for those who were fleeced.

Fortunes were made in selling outfits to would-be prospectors and in providing transportation. Unseaworthy old crates were pressed into service for the first leg of the voyage from the West Coast. Thousands had harrowing experiences on these floating coffins, and many ships never got started or completed only part of the long voyage from Seattle. Plenty of gold was taken out of the Yukon at the height of the gold rush, an estimated $10 million in 1898 alone. But considerably more was spent on transportation and equipment.

At least a million Americans prepared to go to the Yukon. Most of them didn't know where Alaska was, much less the nearby Canadian Yukon. They had little idea how to get there. But they knew that there was gold there by the fistful and the suitcaseful, gold enough for everyone — or so they thought. At least 100,000 actually started on the perilous journey. Perhaps 30,000 to 40,000 actually got to Dawson, the capital of the Klondike.

Throughout the summer and fall of 1897 Canadian and United States officials issued repeated warnings against trying to get to Dawson that year. It was too late in the season to travel safely on either of the two major routes to the Klondike. But the warnings were ignored — at heavy cost.

One route was by ship to St. Michael's on the Bering Sea and then by river steamer 1700 miles up the Yukon to Dawson. But the river froze early and stayed frozen until the spring thaw. The other route, shorter but more difficult and dangerous, was by ship to Skagway in southeast Alaska, then by steep trail to mountain lakes, by boat to the Yukon, and finally along the river to Dawson.

In the cold, bitter fall and winter of 1897, some 5000 prospectors actually tried to cross the mountain trail from Skagway. Many died on the way from hunger or cold. Others were buried in sudden avalanches. After they

crossed the pass, they found that the Yukon had frozen over and that they had come too late. Only a few made it to Dawson — to be told that there was no food for the mushrooming population and that they had to turn back.

The White Pass, the trail most frequently used, became known as the Dead Horse Trail because of the horses — usually old and sickly nags passed off on cheechako prospectors — that died on the way. Jack London, an ex-sailor who joined the gold rush without ever finding gold but whose books about Alaska later made him rich and famous, vividly described the scene:

The horses died like mosquitoes in the first frost. . . . They died at the rocks, they were poisoned at the summit, and they starved at the lakes; they fell off the trail, what there was of it, and they went through it; in the river they drowned under their loads or were smashed to pieces against the boulders. . . . Men shot them, worked them to death and when they were gone went back to the beach and brought more. Some did not bother to shoot them, stripping the saddles off and the shoes and leaving them where they fell. Their hearts turned to stone — those which did not break — and they became beasts, the men on the Dead Horse trail.

Not until the next spring or summer did most of those who had gotten as far as Skagway finally reach Dawson. By that time the swarming mining town had a population of 18,000, with thousands more panning gold in the area; Dawson had almost as many people as the Seattle or Portland of those days.

In one respect at least, Dawson was quite unlike the frontier towns of the American West. The law was strictly enforced by the tough, hardworking Northwest Mounted Police. Free-shooting, two-gun men were strictly out of bounds. So many pistols were confiscated by the police that they were auctioned off at a dollar each as souvenirs.

Goods of other kinds remained scarce, and their prices were high. A man who brought some chickens to Dawson sold his first eggs for a dollar apiece. Nails sold for eight dollars a pound. One cigar salesman made a fortune peddling ten-cent cigars at a dollar and a half each. Many enterprising men, and some women too, made their money not by prospecting for gold but by going into business.

There were a number of courageous women who survived all the rigors of life on the trails and in the tough frontier communities to run successful hotels and stores.

One of the intrepid drivers over the White Pass — the

Dead Horse Trail described by Jack London — was Mrs. Harriet Pullen, a handsome, red-haired widow. She had lost her ranch in Washington state and had four young children to support. Her cook suggested she go to Alaska. Arriving in Skagway with seven dollars, she went to work as a cook, soon discovered an insatiable appetite for the homemade pies she concocted out of dried apples in pans banged out of old tin cans. When she had enough money, she sent for the horses she had managed to save from her ranch and drove miners and their equipment by day and cooked pies at night. Soon she opened a restaurant and a hotel in Skagway and later acquired a fine truck farm. Mrs. Pullen continued to run her hotel long after the gold rush subsided and lived on to a ripe old age.

Thousands poured over the trails (later in the comparative comfort of the White Pass & Yukon Railroad) to Dawson. A few of the newcomers made their stake. But most had no experience as miners or outdoorsmen. Besides, they came after the claims were taken. For most it was a time of hardship and suffering which only later acquired a romantic glow.

Some of the old-time sourdoughs died penniless. A few struck it rich, but even these were often stalked by tragedy. Joe Ladue, a veteran prospector and trader, had gone in search of gold so that he could marry his sweetheart, Anna Mason, and overcome the objection of her wealthy parents. He succeeded beyond his wildest dreams, becoming the richest man in the Yukon. He returned to the states and married the girl; her parents were more than glad to have him now. But it was too late. He died soon afterward, his health undermined by the hardships he had endured in the wilderness. Fires and a variety of misfortunes dogged others who made their pile in the Yukon.

Joe Juneau, who started the original smaller gold rush

in southeast Alaska, wound up running a small restaurant in Dawson. George Carmack, whose discovery at Bonanza Creek was the signal for the Klondike stampede, claimed that he made only a few thousand dollars. One of the richest of the Klondikers, known as the Lucky Swede, died many years later as a saw-mill worker earning $3.25 a day. Another short-time millionaire had to make a living peddling water.

The dream of countless thousands about quick and easy fortune in the Yukon simply did not come true. Many suffered, many died, many never found gold, many lost what they did find. But time mellowed the anguish of the bitter, hungry winters on the trails, and the writings of Robert Service, Jack London, and Rex Beach commemorate the more romantic and dramatic aspects of the years of the gold rush.

Service wrote about "The Spell of the Yukon" — and the Yukon did exercise a magic spell, even on those it defeated and humbled. While many veterans of the hectic days of '97 and '98 left the North never to return, many were drawn to Alaska for life. They could not resist the challenge to conquer the wilderness and wrest treasures from its streams and mountains.

Alaska, so close to the Klondike, benefited substantially from the gold rush. Its population grew rapidly. By 1900 there were more than 30,000 white people in Alaska compared to less than a tenth that number only a few years earlier. The search for gold in Alaska was intensified and several important discoveries were made. Coal and iron mines were developed. New business enterprises sprang up.

The gold rush stimulated at least mild congressional interest in Alaska. In 1898 a homestead law, although an inadequate one, was passed, and the following year Alaska was given a criminal code modeled on Oregon law. In

1900 Congress strengthened Alaska's civil government somewhat by providing for three federal judges (instead of one) to administer justice in that whole vast domain and by increasing salaries of officials. Alaska was still designated a district and still had no elected representation of any kind. The capital was moved to Juneau in 1906. Alaska's long night of neglect was not yet over. But at least the time had passed when Congress could pretend the region didn't exist and most Americans could say they had never heard of it.

9

THE SAGA OF SOAPY SMITH

THE booming town of Skagway, gateway to the trails leading to the Yukon, was swept with a fever of patriotism when the United States got into the Spanish-American War in 1898. And nobody in Skagway was more patriotic than Jefferson Randolph Smith, a distinguished Southern gentleman with a pointed Vandyke beard, who always wore a white silk shirt with a big diamond stickpin.

A man with proud military bearing who was called "Colonel" by his friends, Smith led Skagway's great parade on May 1 to support the nation's war effort. Mounted on a white horse, he waved his sombrero at the crowd of more than 20,000 massed along the city's muddy main street. Many wore brightly colored badges which read *Freedom for Cuba! Remember the* Maine! *Compliments of Skagway Military Company, Jeff R. Smith, Captain.*

A few days after the outbreak of war, Smith announced that he had been appointed Captain of Company A of the 1st Regiment of the Alaska National Guard. He wrote to President McKinley offering to lead a contingent of Alaska Rough Riders to Cuba. When he got back a polite letter rejecting his offer but thanking him for his noble sentiments, this was generally taken as evidence of the high esteem in which he was held in the capital.

Captain Smith set up a tent with the sign *United States Army Recruiting Station*. Into the tent streamed scores of volunteers, bearded miners who abandoned their dreams of fortune and poured back from the Yukon to serve their country. They were signed up by a uniformed officer, ordered to disrobe, examined by an efficient doctor. It all looked very official. The only trouble was that after they left the tent they invariably discovered that their gold dust and other valuables were missing.

There was, of course, no Alaska National Guard. The officer who signed up the miners was no officer, the doctor no doctor. And Captain Smith was no military man. He was the notorious bad man of Skagway, the master criminal who has gone down in history as "Soapy Smith."

The name dates back to one of Smith's early exploits in the mining towns of Colorado. He would show the miners a bar of shaving soap wrapped in a twenty-dollar bill which he offered to sell them for five dollars. Many bought the bars of soap. But none ever found the elusive twenty.

Soapy always claimed that he came from one of the South's first families. Whether he did or not has been disputed by historians. But it is apparently a fact that he was born in Georgia in about 1860, drifted into Texas, and got to Colorado by driving cattle along the Chisholm Trail.

Once west, he soon became head of the underworld. He got his start by defrauding miners with his soap or with the old shell game — betting them they couldn't guess under which half of a walnut he hid a pea. But this was small-time stuff for Soapy. He expanded his operations and opened a highly successful gambling house in Denver, specializing in crooked games.

When he was haled before the Denver Fire and Police

Commission, he talked his way out by explaining that his gambling house was actually an educational institution set up to inform the public about the evils of gambling. He even had a sign on the wall announcing *Let the Buyer Beware*. A learned man, Smith had the sign lettered in Greek and unfortunately not too many of his customers were familiar with the language of Homer. "I should be praised as a public benefactor," he said. "Praise, instead of censure, should be our portion."

When gold was discovered in the Yukon, Smith quickly realized that this was his great opportunity. He left at once for Seattle and got to Skagway before the main influx of gold-seekers. In Seattle he made an interesting offer to an old friend who was a former policeman: "I'm going to be the boss of Skagway. I know exactly how to do it, and if you come along, I'll make you chief of police."

Before settling on Skagway, Smith had considered several other possibilities. He rejected the Canadian Yukon because of its close and efficient supervision by the Northwest Mounted Police. Alaska, almost totally lacking law-enforcement machinery, was more suited to his purpose. He also knew he would have little competition since Alaska was remarkably free of organized criminal gangs. In fact, one reason Smith is so well remembered in history and legend is that he was Alaska's only significant bad man. His career of violence and deception contrasted sharply with the generally lawful conduct of most of Alaska's prospectors and settlers.

Smith picked Skagway because of its strategic position at the entrance to the Yukon trails. Most prospectors would have to go there to get to the Yukon — and, more important, they would return there laden with gold.

By the summer of 1897, Smith was established in Skagway and his smooth line was paying off. A Presbyterian

missionary on his way to Dawson with funds to establish a church there ran into Smith trying out his shell game on a group of miners. It never occurred to the churchman to suspect the well-dressed, courteous gentleman. He entered the game, and before long was relieved of his funds. An evangelist, who had come to Skagway to organize a church, was steered to Smith by one of his friends. Soapy promptly gave him a contribution of $300 and introduced him to the town's leading businessmen, who threw in another $3000. Unfortunately, some of Soapy's boys took the entire sum away from the preacher later that night.

Soapy relied on organization even more than on his glib tongue. He brought in some of his old cronies from Colorado; with these as a core he gathered around him one of the biggest, most efficient and vicious criminal rings ever known in the United States. At its peak his gang included between two hundred and three hundred men — crooks and confidence men, smooth-talkers, and gunmen. One of his men was the "Reverend" Charles Bowers, who seemed to be the very image of a pious clergyman. Bowers was always giving good advice to cheechakos, warning them against getting entangled with bad company and introducing them to upright citizens such as the Moonfaced Kid,

the Blackjack, the Queen, Yank Fewclothes and other pic-
turesquely named members of Soapy's gang. These "lambs,"
as Smith called his bandits, quickly relieved the newcomers
of surplus cash.

On Smith's payroll were the editor of the local paper,
the deputy U.S. marshal, and the justice of the peace. One
of the reporters on the paper interviewed newcomers to
Skagway and managed to find out how much money they
had. In fact, Smith had men in Seattle and Victoria who
looked over likely prospects before they even got aboard
ship for Skagway. One of Soapy's lambs met every arriving
vessel at Skagway to help carry the visitors' luggage up-
town, often lightening it in the process.

Soapy placed his men at key points along the trail leading to the Yukon. His highwaymen were usually tipped off
first by Soapy's agents among the prospectors. If they found
it inconvenient to rob a prospector themselves, they would
steer their prospect to Jeff's Place, as his oyster parlor and
saloon was known. There the miner's gold would be taken
away at a crooked poker game or grabbed outright by one
of the lambs.

In addition, Soapy set up various businesses as a front
for large-scale thievery and fraud. His firms included a
Reliable Packers, an Information Bureau, a Merchants'
Exchange, a Cut-Rate Ticket Office, and a telegraph office.
Since Skagway was not connected with any telegraph system, the telegraph office, of course, sent no wires. But
Soapy, nevertheless, guaranteed to send telegrams anywhere in the world for five dollars, and many suckers believed him.

Across the gulf of more than sixty years, Soapy's exploits
sound humorous and ingenious. But this isn't the whole
story. Many miners, nobody knows the exact number, were
murdered on the frozen trails and their bodies robbed of

gold and other valuables. The crimes of Smith's gang were often cruel and heartless.

In the spring of 1898 there was a great avalanche on one of the trails, tumbling down 2500 feet and burying more than sixty prospectors beneath the snow. In this tragedy, one of the most terrible in the history of the Yukon trails, Smith saw another opportunity for loot. He had himself appointed coroner, set up a tent where corpses recovered from the avalanche were brought. There each frozen body was robbed of gold, jewelry, and cash.

Soapy operated so cleverly that he was able to deny knowledge of the crimes committed by his henchmen — the murders, the robberies, and the crooked games in the back room of his saloon. His suave manner enabled him to deceive the unwary. One writer sent by a big San Francisco newspaper to expose Soapy wound up extolling his virtues and reporting that he was one of Skagway's leading citizens who "bitterly resents the imputation that he is a thief and a vagrant." The writer apparently didn't know that Smith collected a 40 per cent take on all the crimes committed in the area.

Increasingly he began to enjoy playing the role of prominent businessman and public benefactor. He started an "adopt-a-dog" campaign, and took in several stray dogs off the street himself. He was reported to be spending several hundred dollars a week on groceries for needy persons. He supported many widows of men lost on the trails — some of them widowed by Soapy's own lambs.

In the beginning, these giveaways were shrewd moves that enhanced his prestige and made it possible for him to continue robbing Skagway. But Pierre Berton, the Canadian historian of the gold rush, writes that in the end Smith began to believe the role he was playing, considering himself a philanthropist and public benefactor.

Soapy's proudest moment came at the July 4 parade in Skagway. He sat on the platform with the governor of Alaska, waving at the crowd. His own personal army, the brightly uniformed Skagway Military Guards, led the parade. Children munched on the candy he gave away and adults drank his free whiskey. He thrived on the acclaim of his fellow citizens and wanted all Skagway to love and respect him.

But July 4, 1898, was already near the end of Smith's one-year career as the uncrowned king of Skagway. There had been vocal, if ineffective, opposition from the beginning. Now it was coming to a head.

The opposition was led by Frank Reid, schoolteacher, surveyor, one-time Indian fighter, and a crack shot. Reid was never afraid to say what he thought of Soapy. Early in 1898 he organized a vigilante movement and called in federal troops to protect Skagway against Smith's bandits. But the lambs quietly dispersed, to return of course as soon as the troops had left. The vigilantes called mass meetings to denounce Smith and posted a notice:

A Word to the Wise should be sufficient. All con men, bunco and sure-thing men and all other objectionable characters are notified to leave Skagway and the White Pass Road immediately and remain away. Failure to comply with this warning will be followed by prompt action.

But Soapy was powerful, and the vigilantes could never be sure whether one of their friends or business associates might not be one of Smith's lambs. Since saloons — there were seventy in a town of 10,000, all illegal — were a major business in Skagway, Soapy was able to line up considerable support.

Besides, Smith was a master at confusing the issue. He sent his own men into Reid's committee to create disunity. Then he organized his own vigilante committee which issued posters announcing: "The business interests of Skagway propose to put a stop to the lawless acts of many newcomers." Smith called a mass meeting of his own against crime and thundered:

> Fellow citizens, we are here to form a real committee, not a half-baked irresponsible committee such as we have been hearing about. We have the support of the business element of Skagway. We deplore present conditions which are caused not by our own people but by riffraff from all parts of the world. We will protect ourselves even at the cost of our lives.

With such tactics Smith divided the community and made Reid's vigilante committee ineffective.

But just as Soapy reached the height of his power came the incident which caused his downfall. It started out as a routine enough affair — the robbing of a miner named J. D. Stewart who deposited a bag of gold dust worth $2700 in a merchant's safe. One of Soapy's lambs persuaded the miner to take his gold dust to Jeff's place to be examined. There a quarrel was provoked, the poke was seized, and Stewart was thrown out into the street. He complained to acquaintances who took the story to Reid's vigilantes.

Skagway started seething with indignation. Sound business sense rather than humanitarian sympathy for the miner's plight was responsible. Stewart was the first prospector on his way out of the Klondike that year. Word started going around that other miners would now avoid Skagway and go back to the states by the long river route to the Bering Sea rather than brave Soapy's gang. Smith heard that the town was aroused — he was furious at this lack of gratitude for all he had done for Skagway. He determined to seek a showdown rather than lay low for a while as some of his associates counseled.

The morning after the robbery Smith ran into Reid and tried to start a fight so one of his men could shoot the vigilante leader down. But Reid, who was unarmed, walked away. Instead of shooting it out, he called a meeting of his vigilante committee at a dock warehouse. Soapy learned about the meeting from one of his spies and walked down to the warehouse accompanied by a bodyguard of about a dozen men.

Smith cradled a double-barrel repeating Winchester rifle in his arm, and two big revolvers hung from his belt. "Chase yourself home to bed," he shouted to the curious who gathered around. Four guards were stationed near the

warehouse, but he brushed them aside and kept on walk-
ing. Reid caught sight of Soapy and shouted, "You can't
go down there." Smith shouted back, "I'm out to get you,
Reid. You have been at the bottom of all my troubles."

As the two adversaries confronted each other, Reid
caught Soapy's rifle with one hand and tried to shoot his
own pistol with the other. The two men wrestled desperately, and Reid seemed to be gaining. "Don't shoot," Smith
shouted frantically. But it was too late. Both men shot at
the same time. Smith was killed at once. Reid lived for a
while, in terrible agony. "I'm badly hurt, boys," he told
his supporters, "but I got him first."

The angry crowd, supported by infantrymen from nearby Dyea, rounded up Soapy's lambs. The jail was filled
with members of his gang — including such notables as the
editor, the "Reverend" Bowers, and the deputy U.S. marshal. Several were put on trial in Sitka and received prison
sentences of one to ten years. Others were sent back to the
states where they were wanted for a long roster of crimes.

Reid and Smith were buried side by side in the same
graveyard. A wire fence had to be put around Soapy's
grave to protect it from the curious. Legend and the passing of time have been kind to Jefferson Randolph Smith.
He has been remembered as a likable rogue; the murders,
robberies, and other grim deeds have been long forgotten.
But Reid's simple tombstone, with the inscription *He gave
his life for the honor of Skagway,* was neglected.

10

NOME'S GOLDEN BEACH

Hundreds of miles away from the Klondike across the breadth of Alaska was an area of barren arctic prairie known as Cape Nome. It was there, in the extreme west of Alaska facing the Bering Sea, that gold was next discovered. This was a place that had attracted little attention before. Even its name was an accident. On a rough British map it was simply marked *?name,* meaning that it had no name, but the draftsman inking in the map misread the notation and wrote it as Cape Nome.

That part of western Alaska was only thinly settled by Eskimos and Indians. There were a few reindeer herders from arctic Lapland who had been brought in by Sheldon Jackson to teach the Eskimos how to raise the reindeer for food and clothing, and there were also some Norwegian and Swedish prospectors attracted to the area by rumors of gold. In September 1898, a group of these Lapp herders and Scandinavian miners found gold at a stream called Anvil Creek, three miles from the sea.

With their discovery they started a gold rush even more violent and lurid than the one that had engulfed the Klondike. They set in motion a train of events which for a time made Nome the greatest as well as the most lawless and strife-torn mining town in Alaska. In their efforts to mine the gold at Anvil Creek, these obscure prospectors found themselves locked in virtual civil war with other miners and in conflict with some of the most powerful and unscrupulous men in the United States.

Soon after gold was found, prospectors started pouring into the area from all over Alaska and the Canadian Yukon. A crude, rough mining town, called Anvil City at first and later Nome, sprang up. From the outset there were not as many rich claims as the prospectors had hoped for. The best locations had been taken over by the Lapp and Scandinavian discoverers of Anvil Creek.

That winter there was angry talk around the hot Yukon stoves in the cabins of miners who had come to Nome in search of sudden wealth. There were some who convinced themselves that they had found gold at Anvil Creek first. They began to mutter that it wasn't fair for a bunch of foreigners to grab the best claims, and a scheme was hatched to take away their property by force. Disgruntled miners called a meeting and prepared to pass a resolution declaring all claims void and throwing the ground open to new claims. At a signal from the meeting, some of their confederates were to gather on Anvil Mountain and seize the disputed property. But federal troops from St. Michael's intervened and broke up the meeting before the plan could be carried out.

At this point there was a startling new development. Gold was found on the Nome beach. The discovery was heralded in headlines, and to thousands of people all over the United States who read the news, Nome seemed to be the promised land. What could be easier, they thought, than scooping up the gold from the beach?

Steamship companies ran ads announcing that the beach was packed solid with gold along an area 20 to 25 miles

Ahqupuk

wide and 250 miles long. The ads even described how "gold clung to the ship's anchors when they were drawn up." Thousands of men were drawn to Nome by this publicity. They were packed like sardines into every available ship.

The steamship companies made a fortune, charging $125 for one-way passage. But the would-be miners did not fare as well. There was gold on only a narrow strip of beach about three quarters of a mile long, where the fortunate could make from five to ten dollars a day sifting the gold from the sand. There were richer takings in the tundra back of the beaches — but there the gold had to be thawed out, and this took a lot of hard work and coal at $150 a ton.

Such unpleasant facts, however, failed to stop the stampede to Nome. The beaches were crowded for fifteen miles with the tents of prospectors, and the city teemed with angry, restless men who felt cheated and resentful and had little to do except drink in the numerous saloons and get into trouble.

Men were shot in the middle of town in broad daylight, and no arrests were made. Prices were sky-high. Nome's two muddy, unpaved streets didn't even have a ditch or a sewer for refuse. Inevitably disease spread; there were epidemics of smallpox, typhoid, pneumonia.

At best the situation was explosive. The rich claims of the Lapps and Scandinavians became the focal point of mounting resentment. The claim-jumping prospectors who wanted the mines for themselves organized and hired a group of shrewd lawyers. Direct action to seize the mines hadn't worked. Now the idea was to use legal trickery — and high-powered politics in Washington.

The laws governing Alaska provided that aliens could own land. But the claim-jumpers schemed to change the laws to make the holdings of the Lapps and Scandinavians illegal. They sent a lawyer to Washington to lobby for this change; he enlisted the support of Alexander McKenzie, who became the real force behind the struggle to oust the owners from the Anvil Creek mines.

McKenzie was an important politician and Republican national committeeman from North Dakota. He was close to President McKinley and had influential friends in the Senate. Under McKenzie's direction, the battleground shifted from the muddy streets and the boisterous saloons of Nome to the halls of Congress.

Legislation was introduced in the Senate the passage of which would have ousted the Lapps and Scandinavians from their property. Behind the scenes was the aggressive McKenzie, a man big both in size and power. He pulled wires, lined up supporters. The charges and countercharges traded on the Senate floor were scarcely more polite than those which had resounded in Nome. One day the language used in the Senate was so unsenatorial that an issue of the *Congressional Record* had to be withdrawn from circulation. The bitter words were toned down and the issue was reprinted.

McKenzie was blocked in the Senate. But he came up with another scheme — to make himself the principal owner of the best mining claims in Nome. He organized a corporation called the Alaska Gold Mining Company and named himself president and general manager. This company took over the seemingly worthless claims to the Anvil Creek mines of the disgruntled miners who got shares of stock in return. McKenzie proposed to make these claims very valuable indeed by having them recognized as valid and legal by the government. To achieve this end he had to take over the machinery of the courts and law enforcement in Nome. For a time McKenzie succeeded in doing so.

Key man in this daring plan of McKenzie's was Arthur H. Noyes, an old political crony of his from Minnesota. McKenzie persuaded President McKinley to make Noyes United States judge in Nome. He also maneuvered the appointment of his henchmen as U.S. marshal and district attorney. Even the minor posts in Nome went to McKenzie stooges.

So McKenzie sailed from Seattle with a retinue of accomplices including a United States judge. At Nome he left Judge Noyes aboard ship for a couple of days when he went ashore to line things up for the big takeover. With the top government officials in Nome safely in his pocket, it seemed to McKenzie that it would be a snap to wrest the Anvil Creek mines away from a group of Lapp reindeer herders and Scandinavian miners.

At first everything went according to plan. The claim-jumpers, now controlled by McKenzie, took their case before Judge Noyes, claiming to be the rightful owners and naming the real owners as defendants. Noyes appointed McKenzie receiver for the mines. In effect, the judge took the mines away from the men who discovered and developed them and gave them to McKenzie. He instructed McKenzie to take immediate possession and to start digging out the gold.

But McKenzie underestimated his opposition, which was led by two determined and resourceful men. One was Jafet Lindeberg, a former reindeer herder who proved to be a stubborn and resourceful businessman and did not propose to be pushed around by anyone. The other was Charles D. Lane, a hard-boiled prospector and frontiersman who threw in his lot with the Lapp and Scandinavian miners. Lane organized the dispossessed miners and brought in two able young attorneys from San Francisco to fight the issue through in the court.

The first move was to appeal to Judge Noyes to reconsider his decision. But Noyes refused even to listen to an appeal. So the attorneys went to the higher United States Court in San Francisco. There a judge, outraged by the high-handed proceedings in Nome, ordered McKenzie to restore the mine property to its owners and also directed Judge Noyes to stay out of the controversial case in the future.

But McKenzie and Noyes defied the appeals court. They were in a race against time. Winter was fast approaching, and soon Nome would be cut off from the states. If McKenzie could only hold on to the mines a little longer, he would be able to take out a fortune in gold before Nome would be opened up again in the spring.

The attorneys for the embattled miners went to San Francisco once more. This time the judges sent their marshal to arrest McKenzie and enforce their orders. But McKenzie still refused to turn over the mines or the gold he had stored in safety deposit boxes in the Nome bank. With the aid of federal troops, on hand to subdue resistance, the marshal finally broke into the gold-laden boxes, arrested McKenzie, and brought him back to San Francisco.

McKenzie was sentenced to jail for one year, but his term was shortened by President McKinley. Judge Noyes was removed from the bench, found guilty of contempt and fined $1000. The court said: "The high-handed and grossly illegal proceedings initiated almost as soon as Judge Noyes and McKenzie had set foot on Alaska territory . . . may be safely and fortunately said to have no parallel in the jurisprudence of this country."

But Nome was still in chaos. There was no effective law-enforcement machinery at all for a while. McKenzie and Noyes were gone. But the claim-jumpers still held possession of the mines. The Lapp and Scandinavian miners had battled their case patiently through the courts. Now their patience ran out. They descended with guns on the mines and drove off the claim-jumpers and their employees and supporters. In the pitched battle at the mines one of the jumpers was seriously injured. The military moved in and took over the mines.

Eventually, the Lapp herders and Scandinavian miners won in the courts and recovered their property. Law and order were slowly restored in boisterous Nome. The corrupt officials were cleaned out. In 1899 and 1900 alone almost $7 million in gold was taken out of the area.

But the battle for the Anvil Creek mines was not quickly

forgotten. Rex Beach wrote a novel about it called *The Spoilers*. Hollywood made an exciting movie telling the story. For many throughout the United States the violence and drama increased the glamour of Nome as a city where strong men battled over the gold creeks and beaches. But within one man at least, the story of Nome strengthened a growing determination to help bring law and order and self-government to Alaska. This was Judge James Wickersham, who had replaced Noyes in Nome and helped rid that city of its grafters and crooks.

11

ALASKA'S WICKERSHAM

For a few men like Soapy Smith and Alexander McKenzie Alaska was a place to get rich quickly by fraudulent schemes. But for thousands of other men and women, Alaska was not only the land of gold and opportunity but also the land they came to love. They settled there and called it home. They wanted to build it up, remove the roadblocks to its growth, make it part of the United States in every way. For these people James Wickersham served as spokesman for almost forty years, and Alaska's eventual achievement of statehood owed much to his efforts.

Wickersham was born in Patoka, Illinois, in 1857. He became a lawyer and then moved west to Tacoma. Active in local politics, he was elected to the House of Representatives of the new state of Washington in 1898. But he was not always tactful or polite to those he disagreed with, and he antagonized a number of prominent and influential people in the Pacific Northwest. They were interested in getting him as far away from Tacoma as possible.

His enemies rather than his friends were really responsible for getting Wickersham appointed a United States judge in Alaska. Their first move was to urge his appointment as Consul General to Japan on the ground that he was too able a man to keep at home. This proposal reminded him of an old story about how Lincoln had gotten rid of an insistent office-seeker.

A neighbor of Lincoln's from Springfield, Illinois, wanted in the worst way to become an American consul abroad. His qualifications were nonexistent. But Lincoln, worn down by endless entreaties, finally agreed to give him a job. When Secretary of State Seward asked where he should send this unpromising addition to the diplomatic corps, the President stretched his long arm halfway around his biggest office globe and pointed a bony forefinger at the area farthest from Washington. "Send him here," Lincoln said.

Wickersham didn't want to go to Japan. However, his reaction was quite different when he heard it was being suggested that he be sent to Alaska as a federal judge. The appointment appealed to the frontiersman in Wickersham. He loved hunting, mountain climbing, and the outdoor life. Besides, his studies of the American Indians had interested him in Alaska. Wickersham was one of the first to advance the theory that the Indians had come to America from Asia, probably by land across the Bering Strait into Alaska.

He enthusiastically accepted the appointment even after he discovered that he was being sent not to one of the booming gold towns but to an obscure trading post on the upper Yukon with the grand-sounding name of Eagle City. Wickersham's judicial district was big enough; it was 2000 miles wide at one point and included more than half the territory of Alaska. But it was a sparsely populated region, as yet untouched by the gold rush in the Canadian Yukon, only a few miles across the border.

When he got to Eagle, Wickersham discovered that the so-called business section consisted of a few log cabin stores and saloons. After building a log cabin for the use of his family, he raised the funds for a log court house by collecting license fees from each of the five saloons in Eagle. The primitive conditions didn't bother him. Wickersham boasted that he had one of the best and warmest cabins in town. It was always comfortable, even when the temperature outside was sixty degrees below zero.

Wickersham's first case concerned the chief of the Charley River band of Athapaskan Indians. The old chief came up the Yukon in a birch-bark canoe, accompanied by a dozen other Indians, each in his own canoe. He was looking for the big chief of the white men. Chief Charley was sent first to the clerk of the court, then to the marshal, finally to the judge. Looking Wickersham right in the eye, he asked, "You big chief here?" The judge admitted he was. The Indian wanted to know if Wickersham was the biggest chief. Again the judge conceded he was the man. Finally, the old Indian stated his business. His dog had been stolen by the nearby Eagle Indians.

The judge acted with the same solemnity as Chief Charley. He instructed a deputy marshal to proceed to the village and bring back the dog at once. A battle between the Eagle and Charley River peoples was thus averted. Wickersham later discovered that each of Chief Charley's braves had a gun hidden in his canoe. Nor was the theft as trivial as it might seem. A good sled dog was more important in the Yukon than a good horse in the Old West. So Chief Charley went away satisfied. Wickersham established himself at the outset as a big chief who made good his word.

The law was rough and ready in those days on the Yukon. Miners' meetings administered a crude justice, which the prospectors were often prepared to enforce at gunpoint. Judges and courts were something new in Alaska. But generally Wickersham had no trouble with the miners.

He treated them fairly and soon got a reputation as a square-shooter.

The nearest jail was at the mining camp called Circle City. Over the door of the jail, known as the "skookum house" in Indian vernacular, was this announcement: "Notice: All prisoners must report by 9 o'clock P.M. or they will be locked out for the night. By order of the U.S. Marshal." The rule was completely effective. Trying to escape from Circle in weather of thirty or more below zero was not an enticing prospect.

After a while, Wickersham felt he wasn't being kept busy enough with legal business in the Yukon area. Restless for more activity, he wrote to Washington offering to assist the federal judges in Juneau and Nome, who were overloaded with all kinds of mining litigation. He received instructions to lend a hand to Judge Noyes, whose name was about to become notorious in connection with the Nome claim-jumping scandal.

Wickersham's orders, however, took him not to Nome but far out in the Aleutians, which were also in Noyes' division. He was directed to proceed to Unalaska and conduct the first murder trial ever held in the history of the foggy, stormswept islands. The trial was held in a large room over the Alaska Commercial Company's bath house and laundry on the island of Unalaska.

A sailor named Fred Hardy was charged with murdering three prospectors on Unimak Island. One of the three was Cornelius Sullivan, who had made and lost a fortune from the famous Bunker Hill and Sullivan lode mines in Idaho. Sullivan and his companions went to Unimak to find another fortune. But shortly after setting up their camp, Sullivan and two others were murdered. The only survivor, crazed and half-starving, was found by other prospectors on the island and led a search party to three skeletons — the remains of the murdered men.

Hardy seemed to have a strong alibi. Only one witness could possibly break down his story: an ancient Eskimo chief from a fish camp on Unimak, who hardly cut an impressive figure. He seemed senile, was dressed in ragged clothes, smelled of fish, spoke only broken English. Besides, the old chief's story seemed to have a fatal flaw. He said he was sure of the date involved because "me lote it in me log."

The defense attorney walked over to the old Eskimo and said contemptuously, "So you can write, can you? Well, come over here and let the jury see you write." There was a hushed silence in the courtroom. The chief, who could barely speak English, surely couldn't write it. But he shuffled up to a table facing the jury and without hesitation wrote his name clearly and legibly — in Russian. The overeager defense attorney had forgotten about the Russian mission schools which had existed long before the United States purchased Alaska. Hardy was hanged shortly afterward in the first legal execution in that part of Alaska.

The murder trial over, Wickersham prepared to return to Eagle. But just before he sailed a United States warship steamed into Dutch Harbor with peremptory orders from Washington that he proceed to Nome and take over the court there. Judge Noyes' term had ended in disgrace with the exposure of his attempts to turn over the rich Anvil Creek mines to Alexander McKenzie.

Wickersham found the Nome court in chaos. There was no confidence in the crowded boom town that justice could be had in the courts. Many of the prospectors were so disgusted with Noyes' backstairs deals with attorneys that they talked about taking the law into their hands. But

Wickersham calmly convened his court. He assured the military that the civil authorities could control the situation. He decreed an end to backstairs justice. He removed the grafters from office. He quickly cleaned up a big backlog of litigation. Wickersham restored order in Nome. But he also made influential enemies in Alaska and in Washington. McKenzie was still a man to reckon with.

Powerful Alaska mining interests with friends in Washington were antagonized by a number of Wickersham's decisions. In those days a number of members of Congress had investments in Alaskan gold and copper which gave them more than an academic interest in the territory's affairs. As a result, Wickersham was investigated repeatedly by government agents. The judge may have been prickly and irritating. But he was honest. The investigations turned up nothing. This did not, however, stop the sniping. McKenzie and other promoters appeared at Senate Judiciary Committee hearings to oppose his appointment as a judge. Enough senators were impressed to block his confirmation.

But President Theodore Roosevelt kept giving him recess appointments. T. R. developed a loyalty and affection for Wickersham which the judge fully reciprocated. Here were two men with common robustness, common love for the outdoors, common interest in conservation, common opposition to what they considered the immoral practices of some big corporations (or *trusts,* as they were called at that time). As a result of repeated battles over his confirmation, the unknown judge from Tacoma became a national figure.

Wickersham remained in office seven years, something of a record for judges in Alaska in those days. He heard criminal cases and mining cases, performed marriages, officiated at funerals; once he had to make the coffin to bury a pioneer woman who died in the wilderness.

On little trips between court terms, he used to combine hunting white mountain sheep and prospecting for gold. His luck with the sheep was excellent. Once he poked around in the area where an Italian miner named Felix Pedro made a rich strike and where the present city of Fairbanks is located. He was not impressed. Wickersham discovered no gold, but he organized the city government of Fairbanks and later moved his court there. He also founded and wrote the Fairbanks *Miner,* the first newspaper ever published in that part of Alaska. The printing press he used was a typewriter, but the paper sold for five dollars a copy.

After helping establish the city of Fairbanks, Wickersham felt it was time to look around and consider what to do next. It seemed to him that "the most interesting object on the horizon was the massive dome that dominates the valleys of the Tanana, the Yukon and the Kuskokwim, the monarch of North American mountains — Mt. McKinley." So he organized an expedition, the first to attempt climbing the great mountain.

Wickersham and his companions climbed about 12,000 feet before they were defeated by the glaciers and the sheer rock walls. But their achievements were many. They col-

lected ancient Athapaskan Indian legends on their way to
the mountain. They explored territory never before entered
by white men and corrected common geographic errors.
Wickersham made an accurate map of the area. Out of the
trip also came Wickersham's interest in promoting Mount
McKinley National Park, one of the nation's truly fabulous
recreation areas.

Varied as were Wickersham's interests, he became increasingly preoccupied with the cause of self-government.
The judge was convinced that Alaska would someday be
a prosperous and well-populated state. But at every hand
he saw evidence that important people in Washington were
indifferent or even hostile to the aspirations of Alaska's
hardy pioneers. As he had noted during the Nome scandal,
there was considerable interest in getting hold of some of
Alaska's natural wealth. There was all too little, however,
in granting her people the rights of American citizenship.

Alaska had no elected officials, no legislature of its own.
Not until 1906 were Alaskans permitted to elect a delegate
to Congress. That delegate was allowed to introduce bills
and make speeches — but not to vote. What Wickersham
wanted was an elected government in Alaska and real representation in Washington.

In 1907, while he was still a judge, Wickersham made
a speech denouncing "a system of government insufficient
and unsatisfactory to the people of Alaska." The speech
caused a sensation in Alaska and raised eyebrows in Washington. A few months later Wickersham resigned his judge-
ship. In 1908 he ran for delegate from Alaska and was
elected.

The slogan of that campaign, and of several to come,
was "The Wicks *vs.* the Guggs." The Wicks were, of course,
the Wickersham supporters. The Guggs were the villains
of Alaska politics for almost a generation. The term was

the popularly used nickname for the extensive Guggenheim-Morgan interests and for the Alaska Syndicate they had organized. Wickersham and his friends believed that the syndicate dominated the Alaska economy, owning rich copper mines, a railroad, a steamship line, salmon canneries, gold properties. They maintained that the syndicate was opposed to T. R.'s conservation policies and was despoiling the territory's rich natural resources, that it thwarted Alaska's economic and political development and opposed the election of a full-scale territorial government. The Alaska voters apparently believed these charges. They repeatedly elected Wickersham.

While serving in Washington, Wickersham was galled by evidence of contempt for Alaska and her delegate to Congress. His first bill provided for an elected legislature. But President Taft proposed instead that Alaska be ruled by an appointed commission under the Bureau of Insular Affairs. Early in 1910, Wickersham was tipped off by a friendly senator that this scheme had been introduced as a bill at the President's request by Senator Albert Beveridge, chairman of the Senate Committee on Territories and that secret hearings on the measure were then taking place.

Wickersham stalked across the hall to the committee room and knocked on the closed door.

An attendant opened the door a few inches and informed him: "The committee is in session, and you can't come in."

"But I'm the delegate from Alaska," Wickersham protested, "and I wish to see Senator Beveridge."

"Yes, sir," the attendant replied, "but he told me not to let you in."

Wickersham put his foot in the crack of the door and pushed his way in.

As he walked to the committee table, Beveridge said

sharply: "Mr. Delegate, the Committee is in session, and I cannot see you."

"But Mr. Chairman," Wickersham replied, "I am informed by a member of this committee that the Alaska Government bill is now under consideration by the committee, and I wish to be heard before it is reported."

Wickersham was heard. The committee overruled its chairman. The Beveridge bill was defeated. Two years later Congress passed a bill fathered and steered by Wickersham. This was the Act of 1912 giving Alaska an elected legislature — the act which substantially determined the form of Alaska's government until statehood was achieved in 1958. Passed in a form far more restrictive than Wickersham desired, it still left Alaska with an appointed governor and with control from Washington over its resources and many of its problems. Besides, it denied Alaska effective representation in Congress. But for all that, the law of 1912 was an important step forward on the road to self-government and constituted one of Wickersham's greatest achievements.

For six consecutive terms the people of Alaska elected Wickersham their delegate to Congress, and then later in the depression of the 1930s, when he was an old man, he was elected for a seventh term. There were always important groups in Alaska which fought him bitterly. He was denied certificates of election for two of his seven terms although both times the House of Representatives declared him legally elected.

In Washington his years were stormy. He was up against influential personal and political enemies and was opposed by strong lobbies which combated the legislation he introduced on behalf of Alaska. The lack of interest in Alaska, general in Washington and in the country as a whole, made it difficult to get things done.

Ahgupuk

But Wickersham kept plugging away and sponsored other significant legislation in addition to the 1912 law. To him belongs much of the credit of providing for construction of the government-built and -operated Alaska railroad, creating the Alaska Agricultural College and School of Mines (which subsequently became the University of Alaska), and establishing Mount McKinley National Park.

Perhaps his most important bill was one that wasn't passed until many years after his death in 1939. On March 30, 1916, he wrote in his diary: "Introduced the first Alaska Statehood Bill today." In 1910 he had written an article titled "The State of Alaska: The Forty-Ninth Star."

Always he was sustained by what he called a vision of

the future of Alaska. He foresaw "a land of happy homes; of farms and bounteous crops; of towns and flourishing cities; of roads and railways; of schools and troops of happy children; of colleges filled with students; of churches and pious worshippers; of mines and factories — a land of strong men and women who would erect there a sovereign state in the American Union." He fought bravely and well to make that vision come true. Little known in the other forty-nine states, Wickersham is regarded in Alaska as the father of statehood. That is why Alaskans generally consider him their state's first citizen.

12

LOCKING UP THE TREASURE

WHO could say after the gold rush that Alaska was a barren waste and its purchase a colossal folly?

Out of Alaska poured millions of dollars in gold every year. Its $22-million output in 1906 amounted to more than a fifth of the nation's gold production, surpassing California, second by only a hair to Colorado.

The gold rush spurred the discovery of other minerals. Prospectors found rich copper deposits in the Chitina Valley, and by 1916 Alaska was producing more copper than gold, $30 million worth that year alone. Tungsten ore was located in the Fairbanks area, tin on the Seward Peninsula. Lead, chrome, nickel, cobalt, and molybdenite were found in significant quantities. There were vast coal deposits in many areas of Alaska, particularly in the Matanuska Valley.

But rich as were the mineral resources of Alaska, the value of the fish taken out of its waters became greater than the output of all its mines. In 1917, Alaska's salmon industry did more than $50 million in business, and other fish products added an additional $6 million.

After half a century of American rule, Alaska had far more than repaid the original $7.2 million purchase to the

treasury and was contributing generously to the national wealth. Every year it was exporting about $75 million in products to the United States, importing more than $35 million.

For a few years after the gold rush, Alaska continued to grow and prosper. It seemed that Alaska was on the verge of realizing its promise. But then stagnation and even decline set in.

Alaska's population doubled during the gold rush, reaching a total of almost 65,000 in 1900. The influx of prospectors and would-be prospectors continued for a while. But then thousands began to leave, offsetting the number of the newcomers. When the 1910 census was taken, it showed that there had been virtually no growth compared to 1900. By 1920 the figures told the disastrous story of a 14.7 per cent decline in Alaska's small population.

There was obviously something terribly wrong in Alaska. Why was its population declining at a time when the population of the United States as a whole was increasing rapidly?

Strangely enough Alaska was still suffering from its old affliction — neglect, ignorance, and hostility in Washington. Surely nobody could make the claim any longer that Alaska wasn't worth the time, trouble, and federal appropriations necessary to develop its resources. And yet some did say just that — despite all the facts which proclaimed the contrary.

Alaskans kept explaining patiently that transportation was the key to all their problems. Alaska desperately needed a transportation system which would link its widely separated areas, make it possible to bring goods in and out of the interior, tie Alaska closer to the ports of the United States. It needed roads, railroads, and better steamship service.

But Alaska could get no action from the federal government. Every time it was proposed in Congress to spend some money to help develop Alaska, congressmen would repeat old stories about how all the ground in Alaska was frozen to a depth of at least six feet. In 1914, when an appropriation for Alaska was before the House, a congressman from Georgia asked: "Why send it to the North Pole? Why not spend it at home? Have we so much money, are we so rich, that we would rather send it to the North Pole than send it to the people of our districts? Are we so rich that we can afford to develop Alaska while America languishes?"

Ever since the early days of United States rule, Alaskans complained that steamship service was poor and rates high.

Ahgupuk

The Sitka *Alaskan* protested in 1886 that a man who shipped a seven-dollar table from Portland to southeast Alaska had to pay freight charges of twenty dollars; this situation improved little over the years. High steamship rates made it expensive to ship Alaska's mineral products, and this was one of the factors blocking the development of the economy.

Alaska urgently needed charts of its waterways and the lighthouses along the 26,000-mile coastline. But Congress repeatedly denied appropriations for both. In 1914 a member of the House read off a list of 260 shipwrecks, costing 449 lives, off Alaska's coast. In 1917, after Alaska had been part of the United States for fifty years, only 9 per cent of its coast had been surveyed. As a result, marine insurance rates for ships in the Alaska trade were double those charged for other West Coast ports. This in turn increased transportation costs from Alaska.

The worst blow to Alaska's steamship transportation came in 1920 when Congress passed the Jones Act, requiring that all goods to and from Alaska be shipped in American bottoms. This meant that goods could not be shipped into Alaska from nearby Canadian ports in Canadian ships, but had to be sent to Seattle and then come into Alaska in American vessels. The result was to increase the cost of consumer and industrial products to Alaskans. It was also to strengthen the grip of an existing steamship monopoly, which was now free of any threat of Canadian competititon.

Alaskans trying to set up new businesses were hit hard by the Jones Act. For example, an enterprising resident of Juneau started shipping Alaska's Sitka spruce for the use of the emerging aircraft industry of the Midwest via Vancouver, British Columbia. When the Jones Act required him to ship via Seattle, his costs doubled. He was forced to close down his mill.

Ever since the gold rush, Alaskans had hoped for railroads that would connect them with the United States or at least serve the internal needs of the economy. Several private firms started railroads into the interior but failed for lack of capital. A railroad was built by the copper interests to serve their Kennecott mines, but this was an exception. It became clear through the years that government aid was needed for railroad construction in Alaska.

This project was greeted with hoots of derision whenever it was raised in Congress. A Kentucky congressman opposed "going to Alaska to break the Ice Trust by building a railroad through it." A Georgia congressman attacked the notion of dumping the government's millions "in that frozen and unproductive section." The government had sub-

Ahgupuk

sidized railroads through the West. It was different when it came to Alaska.

In 1914 Congress finally authorized a government-owned railroad in Alaska and appropriated a million dollars to get it started. Even then it dragged its feet in putting up the additional funds necessary, and construction proceeded slowly. The railroad, connecting the port of Seward with Fairbanks in the interior, was finally completed in 1923.

But if Alaskans didn't get a railroad for twenty-five years after the gold rush, why didn't they use roads? The reason is simple. There weren't any — not, at least, at the time they were most needed. A Senate committee which visited Alaska in 1903 reported that there was "not to be found a single wagon road over which vehicles can be drawn summer or winter." The committee recommended federal action. But Congress delayed, and the appropriations finally forthcoming were meager and inadequate. When a federal highway act was passed in 1916, Alaska was excluded from the benefits which went to the states of the union.

Lack of transportation was a major reason for Alaska's failure to develop her economy and use her rich natural resources to the greatest advantage. Without railroads, mining Alaska's coal appeared too expensive. On the other hand, railroads needed cheap coal to operate profitably. Alaska was caught in a vicious circle.

Strange things were happening. Good timber was rotting in Alaska's great forests — while lumber was being brought in from the Pacific Northwest at great cost. Coal was lying unmined in the Matanuska Valley and elsewhere — while coal was being imported from British Columbia.

There was another important reason for this peculiar paradox. The federal government blocked off the use of many of Alaska's resources. Federal regulations prohibited cutting of lumber from public lands, which meant virtually all land in Alaska. One salmon cannery in southeast Alaska was prevented from shipping out its products in barrels and boxes it manufactured at its own mill; it was told it had to import the lumber.

Even more important was the federal freeze on the use of Alaska coal, decreed by President Theodore Roosevelt in 1906, which remained in effect for many years. T. R. acted with the intention of blocking a fraudulent grab of Alaska's coalfields by monopoly interests. He also had in mind the larger view of conserving Alaska's resources, such as lumber and coal, against thoughtless and wasteful exploitation. The coal freeze set a pattern, and in 1910 Alaska's oil lands were closed to private ownership or lease.

While the objectives were praiseworthy, the methods effectively locked up some of Alaska's most valuable natural treasures. Besides, Alaska's forests and mineral reserves could be used for centuries without serious danger of exhaustion.

In any case, Alaska's citizens were being forced to import products they had close at hand. The Alaskans were particularly indignant about the coal freeze, which prevented them both from meeting their own needs and from serving the West Coast of the United States which was long supplied with coal from the East.

Their most forceful protest has gone down in history as the Cordova Coal Party. In 1911 some three hundred citizens of the port of Cordova marched to the Alaska Steamship Company's dock and dumped several hundred tons of coal from British Columbia in imitation of the Boston Tea Party.

The coal controversy raged not only in Alaska; it became a major national issue. It touched off a split in the Republican Party over the conservation policies followed in Alaska. Ardent conservationist T. R. refused to support President William Howard Taft, whom he suspected of being less devoted to the cause. Roosevelt formed his own Progressive Party, and the election of Woodrow Wilson in 1912 as the first Democratic president since Grover Cleveland was the inevitable consequence.

Alaskans were all for the principles of conservation, and by and large they tended to support T. R.'s crusade against monopolies. But they found the application of conservation policies to their territory both rigid and strangely inconsistent.

Wasteful salmon-fishing practices, including use of the fish traps hated by local fishermen and business interests, continued virtually unchecked. The danger of depleting

Ahgupuk

Alaska's salmon resources was real; there was the terrible
example of how the supply of walruses, seals, and whales
and — before that — of sea otters had been virtually destroyed. It seemed curious that the government acted vigorously to conserve coal but did little or nothing to save
the salmon.

Alaskans fared little better under the trust-busting aspect
of T. R.'s program. While monopoly was blocked in coal
by bottling up that resource, it flourished in steamship
transportation, copper, and, to some degree, in salmon
canning.

The conservation muddle was only one of the problems
created in Alaska by contradictory and confusing government policies. Federal agencies had neglected Alaska for

decades. When they started moving in, they did so with such profusion that they throttled the economy in red tape. A citizen interested in leasing an island for fur farming inquired of three government departments, all of which had jurisdiction over some islands. After months of delay, he discovered that none of these could lease him the island he wanted. Bears came under the jurisdiction of three separate departments. Alaskans seeking to establish homesteads or to acquire land also had to run a gamut of conflicting agencies and regulations.

Alaska needed two things from Washington: (1) authority to set up its own government and administer its own affairs and (2) aid in doing those things it could not do itself, chiefly the development of a transportation system. The federal government provided neither. The small measure of self-government wrested from Washington was too weak to do the job. The only effective aid in transportation was the Alaska Railroad, but this came too late to offset the stagnation that had already begun.

So, in the midst of a national treasure of resources, Alaskans were finding in the 1920s that they had no work to do. Metal mining was declining. The canneries employed mainly labor from the northwestern states and California. No new industries were developing. One government official testified in 1921 that many old-timers who had lived in Alaska for years and wanted to stay there were being forced to sell homes at from $50 to $150 "in order to get out of the territory simply because there was no work they could do to earn a living." Another official testified at the same time that Alaska is "on the skids right now." So it seemed. Alaska was being forgotten and neglected again, despite all the excitement of its rediscovery during the gold rush. Yet Alaska turned out to be a place impossible either to neglect or to keep down.

13

TRAIL-BLAZERS

In 1921 Carl Ben Eielson, a slender young man with broad shoulders had a far-away look in his blue eyes, was answering questions at the information desk at the Capitol in Washington. Between questions he sneaked an occasional look into his law books from Georgetown University. But more often than not he was dreaming about his real love — flying.

One day he got into a conversation with Dan Sutherland, the Alaskan delegate to Congress. Sutherland told Ben about a teaching job open at the Fairbanks high school. He also told the young law student about the vast empire to the north which was lying undeveloped because of lack of transportation. It seemed to Ben that Alaska needed planes and flyers more than anything else.

The idea of going to Alaska appealed to him almost at once. He had always been restless, even as a boy in Hatton, North Dakota. He had studied law without much enthusiasm, then enlisted in the air service of the Army in 1917. Although World War I ended just before he was to be shipped overseas, he learned how to fly and was commissioned a lieutenant. After the war, he returned to the study of law. What he really enjoyed, though, was the work he did during summer vacations to earn his tuition — barn-storming in a small plane at fairs and circuses all over the Midwest. Then he wrecked his plane and had just enough money for a ticket to Washington to start his final year of law. Ben had worked hard to put himself through law school. But he didn't really want to be a lawyer.

Ben took the teaching job in Alaska. He knew that the feasibility of flying in Alaska's cold weather had been demonstrated in 1920 by the successful flight, sponsored by General Billy Mitchell, of the Army Black Wolf Squadron from Mineola, New York, to Nome. Eielson was certain that commercial flying had a great future in Alaska and that somehow he would get his chance there.

For a while Ben taught mathematics, general science, and English in a modest red frame building; he also coached the school basketball team. But students noticed that he frequently digressed from the subject at hand to tell them that Fairbanks would one day be square in the middle of the world's great airways, a major center for air transportation between the United States and the Orient.

"I came up here to teach, but what I really want to do is fly," he would tell friends.

In 1923 he persuaded "Wrong Font" Thompson, the editor of the Fairbanks *News-Miner* (who got his nickname from the scrambled type that often appeared in the paper), and Dick Wood, a banker, to help him start the Farthest North Airplane Company. It wasn't much of a company, and it had only one plane. But it was a beginning.

The next year Ben got a contract from the Post Office Department to deliver mail between Fairbanks and Mc-Grath, a distance of about 300 miles. Ben covered the route in three hours — against eighteen days by dogsled. Most of Fairbanks waited anxiously in the ball park for him to

Ahgupuk

return from his first trip. When he arrived — successfully except for some minor damage to the plane when he landed in the park — he was carried on the shoulders of friends to his little hangar where the mayor formally presented him a watch, engraved with "From the citizens of Fairbanks to Ben Eielson, Alaska's Aerial Trail Blazer."

Ben thought he proved that mail delivery by plane was far superior to dogsled in Alaska's interior. But his contract was only for ten twice-a-month round trips to McGrath. Landing on his return from his eighth trip, his wheels got bogged down in the mud of the Fairbanks ball park, and the plane crashed sideways. The Post Office Department refused to pay for repairs. It informed him that the mail delivery experiment "had been successful to a marked degree" but it would be discontinued until the Department could "have an opportunity to study carefully every angle of the situation."

But Ben wasn't going to sit around and wait for that prolonged study. He took off for Washington to try to interest the government in air service for Alaska. He tried to get another mail contract. He also tried to interest the Army in sending military planes to Alaska. When he failed, he spent several months at Langley Field, Virginia, studying advanced flying techniques. He also perfected a new type of ski for heavy planes, an important development for Alaska flying.

Still discouraged about interesting the government in Alaska aviation, he returned to Hatton and went into business with his brother as a bond salesman. Fortunately, he didn't have to sell bonds very long. Captain George Hubert Wilkins, the famous Australian explorer, asked Ben to serve as a pilot on a precedent-breaking expedition to explore the Arctic Ocean by air.

Eielson made three major flights into the Arctic with Wilkins. On one occasion their plane cracked up on an ice island about sixty-five miles northwest of Point Barrow. Stranded for six days in a blizzard, they finally made their way back to land across the frozen ocean. In 1928 Eielson and Wilkins made their historic flight across the North Pole from Point Barrow to Spitsbergen — a twenty-hour flight under difficult flying conditions with primitive instruments; even a compass could not be relied on in the Arctic.

It was a flight fully as significant and spectacular as that of Lindbergh across the Atlantic the year before, and Eielson was greeted as a hero both in Europe and in the United States on his return from Spitsbergen.

Ben got a tremendous ovation all the way back across the country from New York to the hayfield in North Da-

Ahgupuk

kota where he had once flown a little Jenny. He was met by the government and a crowd of 5000. But he brushed aside all the adulation, telling reporters, "Twenty and a half hours and two meals, I guess that's all there was to it. It seems like a mockery to compare our trips in a well-warmed cabin airplane with the hardships other explorers have endured."

Wilkins and Eielson made one more expedition together, this time into the Antarctic; here they discovered land from the sky for the first time, sighting six previously unknown islands.

By this time Ben was acknowledged one of America's greatest pilots. He was given the Distinguished Flying Cross, and President Hoover presented him the Harmon Trophy, the American government's most prized aviation award.

After the triumph of his arctic explorations, he was at last in a position to realize his dream of putting commercial aviation in Alaska on a firm footing. Eielson interested a major New York company in setting up Alaska Airways as a subsidiary, with himself as vice-president and manager and with an air route to the Orient as an ultimate objective.

As his first major assignment on his new job, Ben was asked in 1929 to rescue the passengers and the valuable fur cargo of an American motor ship icebound off North Cape, Siberia. He made one successful trip, but never returned from his second flight to the vessel. A joint American, Canadian, and Soviet rescue expedition, the largest and most elaborate of its time, was organized. The bodies of Eielson and his mechanic, Earl Borland, were recovered on the ice in the shattered wreckage of their plane.

Eielson Air Force Base near Fairbanks and Mount Eielson in Mount McKinley National Park are named after Alaska's pioneer airman, who died at the age of thirty-two. Although he lost his life in the process, Eielson was one of the daring pilots who demonstrated that aviation in the Arctic was practical, that engines operated satisfactorily in cold weather, that landings were possible in snow and ice.

There were many other gallant young men who introduced flying to the far North. There was Joe Crosson, the mercy pilot who saved innumerable miners and trappers stranded in Alaska's interior. There were the Wien brothers — Noel, Ralph, Fritz, and Sig — who barnstormed all over Alaska and later founded one of Alaska's major home-owned commercial airlines. A little later there was Bob Reeve, a pilot who repeatedly landed successfully on glaciers.

These men, flying crude planes without instruments on

unscheduled flights, were called bush pilots. They remain among Alaska's most important heroes. They contributed at least a partial solution to the old and desperate need for transportation. Even if there were few roads and railroad service was limited, planes could go anywhere. And the bush pilots did go anywhere and everywhere. They flew to the most distant native villages and to mines deep in the mountains. They could land anywhere with pontoons or skis, on rivers and lakes, on sandbanks, on ice and snow. Soon Alaskans were no longer isolated. The bush pilots could always take them where they had to go.

Alaskans themselves, with little aid from the federal government to build flying fields and to set up safe airways, established an effective air transportation system. Long before flying became universally accepted in the United States, Alaskans were using planes as a matter of course to get around their vast territory and were shipping everything from mining machinery to chickens, cows, snuff, and canned goods by plane. Alaskans became "the flyingest people under the flag," according to one writer, and by 1939 their planes "were handling twenty-three times as many passengers and a thousand times as much freight, per capita, as the airlines of the United States."

Other pioneers spurred Alaska's unspectacular but steady progress during the thirties. These were the homesteaders and farmers who proved that Alaska was good agricultural country which need not be dependent on the states for its entire food supply and who helped change the national image of Alaska as a frozen waste where no green thing would grow.

Actually there had been solid evidence for a long time that there was plenty of good agricultural country in Alaska, especially in the Matanuska Valley near Anchorage and farther north in the Tanana Valley near Fairbanks.

Traders, trappers, and prospectors who planted gardens there usually got good results.

George Palmer, who had a trading post in the Matanuska Valley, planted some seeds he got in 1900 from Sitka. "Parsnips are the finest and largest I ever saw," he reported. "Turnips grow to an enormous size, and of fine flavor. . . . Rutabagas are large and fine. . . . Lettuce, peas, radishes, cauliflower and potatoes are a success."

Over the years a few venturesome homesteaders established themselves in the fertile Matanuska Valley, protected by a rim of mountains against blizzards and storms. They had many difficulties to overcome — restrictions on homesteading in Alaska, lack of transportation, cost of clearing the land. Most of them had to do mining or other work and farm part time. The coming of the Alaska Railroad through the valley in the 1920s was a help, and the railroad actively promoted colonization of homesteaders late in the decade.

But the first major farming project in Alaska was started in 1935 by President Franklin D. Roosevelt. This was the Matanuska Valley colony, part of the New Deal rural rehabilitation program designed to help needy farmers all over the country. The President directed the setting up of the Alaska Rural Rehabilitation Corporation with these objectives: to help farm families displaced during the depression, many of them on relief; to find out whether Alaska provided a suitable settlement area for what seemed at that time a surplus population plagued by unemployment and poverty; to explore the possibilities of developing Alaska's agriculture.

The colonists, chosen by relief agencies in Minnesota, Michigan, and Wisconsin, were to be financed by the government to buy forty acres of valley land, clear the brush and timber, purchase equipment, and build homes. They were to pay the government back for this aid over a period of years. The program was called subsistence farming. The farmers would produce not for the market but simply to meet their own needs.

In a time of economic depression this idea seemed tremendously attractive. It captured the national imagination and received widespread publicity. Thousands of families were anxious to try it, and those chosen were much in the public eye. They were greeted by bands, met along the way to Alaska by prominent officials, featured in the newspapers.

But there was no flag-waving or hoopla when the two hundred families finally selected got to the freight station on the Alaska Railroad called Palmer. They had to face some grim realities. Housing had not yet been constructed, and the colonists and their children had to live in tents for several months. Epidemics of scarlet fever, measles, and chicken pox spread among the children. There were not enough tractors on hand, and clearing of the land proceeded slowly. There had been faulty judgment in the selection of some colonists, who lacked sufficient farming experience or the temperament to meet obstacles in a new, wild country and had to be sent home.

When the difficulties and snags developed, the reaction in the states was severe. The public turned sharply critical, and the newspapers pilloried the whole program as visionary. But when all the controversy subsided, it turned out that the Matanuska colony was on the whole a substantial and significant success.

Many families stayed and made a go of it. Replacements were found for those who left. Soon the Matanuska colonists were raising cabbages and other vegetables. The cabbages grew to thirty pounds and more in some cases, and six-inch pea pods with huge peas inside were raised. Hay was grown for fodder, and before long there were successful dairy farms in the valley.

A cooperative creamery was established, and Matanuska dairy products became popular over a wide area. The farmers formed their own cooperative association which helped them store and market their products as well as buy more cheaply. Gradually, the subsistence idea was dropped and restrictions on acreage modified. Commercial farming through a cooperative turned out to be a more successful and practical approach.

Life was hard at first, but there were many compensations. For those who loved outdoor life there were salmon in the river, and hunting for mountain sheep and ducks. Women and children could pick blueberries, currants, and

raspberries in the woods. Gradually the colonists were also able to enjoy some of the refinements of civilization. Palmer, the railroad siding where the colonists first arrived, became a flourishing country town with a community center, school, sewage system, garage, post office, electricity, movie theater, and eventually a telephone system.

The Matanuska colony did achieve its major objectives, despite initial difficulties. It helped many midwestern farm families hard hit by the depression. It proved that Alaska was suitable for settlement. And, above all, it proved that agriculture was feasible in Alaska. Old wives' tales, which had circulated for years, that Alaska vegetables were inferior or that Alaska milk had a peculiar taste were shown to be without foundation.

Although the Matanuska experiment was the New Deal's major contribution to Alaska, the territory gained some benefits from other Roosevelt programs. The President's order in 1933 raising the price of gold spurred gold production. Public Works Administration and Works Progress Administration projects gave work to the unemployed and built projects of lasting value such as bridges and schools, playgrounds, fire stations, and paved streets. A hotel was built in Mount McKinley National Park, and Civilian Conservation Corps boys made trails and shelters. Totem poles and other Indian art objects, which had been allowed to deteriorate, were restored by WPA projects. The Roosevelt administration did not, however, remove the many discriminations against Alaska. Inadequate road appropriations were actually cut.

But on the whole Alaska suffered less than most parts of the country during the depression years and even made some advances. Seeking new opportunities, many people — skilled workers, teachers, professionals — came to Alaska during the thirties. Alaska's population, for the first time since 1900, showed a substantial increase over the previous decade. It was 22.3 per cent greater in 1939 than in 1929 and reached a new, although modest, high of 72,000. Alaska was beginning to come out of its long slump on the eve of the dramatic events that were to increase spectacularly the pace of its development.

14

WAR DISCOVERS ALASKA

Eᴀʀʟʏ in 1934 Anthony J. Dimond, the lanky, weatherbeaten ex-gold miner who was then Alaska's delegate to Congress, stood on the rostrum of the House of Representatives in Washington and tried to explain that Alaska was on the shortest invasion route between Japan and the United States.

"Defend the United States by defending Alaska!" Dimond pleaded. "Establish bases at Anchorage or Fairbanks, also in the Aleutians."

That was the year after Hitler had come to power in Germany, and three years after the Japanese war lords had flexed their muscles by invading Manchuria. But nobody paid much attention to Dimond.

The next year Brigadier General William (Billy) Mitchell, the Army's pioneer advocate of air power, appeared before the House Military Affairs Committee to warn: "Japan is our dangerous enemy in the Pacific. They won't attack Panama. They will come right here to Alaska."

Then Mitchell made a statement calculated to startle those congressmen who still thought of Alaska as an unimportant and isolated backwoods area far removed from everything except the North Pole.

"Alaska's the most central place in the world for air-craft," he declared, "and that is true either of Europe, Asia or North America. I believe in the future he who holds Alaska will hold the world, and I think it is the most important strategic place in the world."

Nobody paid much attention to Mitchell either. Year after year, during the 1930s, proposals for air bases and other military installations in Alaska kept coming before Congress — and just as regularly they were knocked out of appropriation bills.

When war came to Europe in 1939, Alaska was totally undefended. The only United States military force in Alaska consisted of two infantry companies armed with Springfield rifles and stationed at Chilkoot Barracks. This antique installation had been built during the gold rush to regulate the traffic of prospectors pouring off the trails from Skagway into the Yukon. It was ideally suited for this purpose. But by 1939 the gold rush was a yellowed page in old scrapbooks, and Chilkoot Barracks was a useless military relic.

As late as March 1940 an economy-minded House Appropriations Committee struck out a $13-million item for an Army air base at Anchorage. When the Japanese struck at Pearl Harbor, not a single base or military installation in Alaska was completed. By that time, however, a submarine base in the Aleutians at Dutch Harbor and a cold-weather testing station for military aircraft were under construction.

After Pearl Harbor the military services began to beef up Alaska's defenses in earnest — and Congress began approving without question appropriations of considerably more than the $7.2 million originally paid for Alaska to construct individual military installments. Naval bases already under way were rushed to completion. The Army built major air bases at Anchorage and Fairbanks. The

Army also began secretly fortifying Alaska's western frontier with bases at Cold Bay on the Alaska Peninsula and
Unimak Island in the Aleutians. As cover for this operation,
the Army had its supplies sent to a nonexistent company
it called Blair and Caxton with mythical canneries on Alaska's west coast. The Alaska Highway, linking the United
States with Alaska through Canada, was begun early in
1942, and in the same year two pipelines were built to
speed up delivery of fuel to our armed forces.

The military buildup of Alaska came just in the nick of
time. The warnings of men like Dimond and Billy Mitchell
were not alarmist. Japan had, in fact, long been preparing
to attack Alaska. All through the thirties the Japanese had
been gathering information about Alaska and the Aleutians.
Japanese fishing vessels, many with naval officers aboard,
had studied western Alaska closely. Japanese weather stations were far better informed than were the inadequate
United States meteorological stations in Alaska on the
stormy and uncertain weather of the Aleutians.

On June 3, 1942, the Japanese attacked. Their Zero
fighters swooped down through the fog at Dutch Harbor,
machine-gunning barracks, warehouses, a radio station, and
Navy flying boats lying idle in the water. The next day the

Japanese returned with carrier-based bombers and more fighters. Fortunately, the Navy rallied and, with the aid of Army planes at the new secretly constructed Unimak Island base, drove off the Japanese, scoring hits on a carrier and several warships.

The Japanese push into the Aleutians was part of a massive two-pronged pincer attack aimed at crippling American defenses in the Pacific in preparation for a possible invasion of the United States. Three hours after the Zeros struck Dutch Harbor, our patrol planes far to the south discovered a great Japanese armada headed straight for Midway Island. Here the United States Navy won one of its decisive victories of World War II, sinking four Japanese aircraft carriers, damaging three battleships, and killing some 5000 men.

While the southern arm of the Japanese pincers was thus nipped off at Midway, the northern arm managed to hang on. Rebuffed at Dutch Harbor, the Japanese captured Attu and Kiska islands. Here they fortified themselves for a long stay, building airfields and pillboxes, laying up enormous supplies of canned and dehydrated foods. Although their main strategy had been thwarted, the Aleutians were still important to Japan as a base from which to attack Alaska

and the United States and, in any event, from which to disrupt the flow of planes and supplies to the Soviet Union via Alaska.

United States Army units, supported by Army and Navy planes, launched a surprise attack from new Aleutian bases to recapture Attu on May 11, 1943. The Japanese fought hard to hold on. They burrowed into the hills and rocks, separated into small units and fought guerrilla style. Our men faced constant fire from invisible snipers. After two months and 1500 casualties that included 400 dead, the United States finally recaptured Attu. Kiska was next on our timetable and was softened up by aerial bombardment. But it fell without a fight; the Japanese secretly evacuated the island a few days before American and Canadian troops landed on August 15.

United States forces fighting in the Aleutian campaign were handicapped by lack of knowledge of the area. Alaskans both in and out of the armed forces helped supply this lack. Many individuals made important contributions. For example, Father Bernard Hubbard, the glacier priest who had explored Alaska widely, lectured to soldiers, helping overcome their fear of fighting in the mysterious Aleutians. He also provided the military with more than a million feet of film on Alaska's geography and helped improvise lightweight, weather-resistant clothing for our forces.

Alaska's men and women rallied to the war effort, virtually all assisting in one capacity or another. More than 7500 men, out of a total population of only 72,000 in 1940, served in the armed forces. Another 4000 served in the Alaska Territorial Guard, formed when National Guard units were federalized. ATG units patrolled vast stretches of Alaska's coast against raiding parties. Alaska's native peoples were intimately familiar with the terrain and

weather, and Eskimos, Indians, and Aleuts played an important role in ATG scout units. Many Eskimo boys under the general enrollment age of sixteen insisted on serving in ATG and were useful in remote areas of the Bering Sea and on arctic coasts.

The hasty buildup of American strength in Alaska not only resulted in the recapture of our islands but turned out to be valuable in the latter phases of the war. From Attu and Kiska the United States was able to bomb Japan's Kurile Islands. Alaska also served as a major supply base for Russia's war effort. Planes for the Soviet Union were readied at Ladd Air Force Base near Fairbanks, from which Russian pilots took off for Siberia.

Whether strong defenses in the Aleutians and on the

mainland of Alaska might have prevented a Japanese attack is a matter of conjecture. It is probable, however, that if we had been better prepared, the occupation of Attu and Kiska by the Japanese could have been averted and casualties substantially reduced. In any case, the United States paid dearly for its long neglect of Alaska and is not likely to repeat this mistake.

Alaska's strategic importance was amply demonstrated. It was shown that Seward had been right when he said Alaska was a bridge between America and Asia. It was important to the United States that we control this bridge. Such pioneers as Colonel Ben Eielson and General Mitchell were proved right in their conviction that Alaska was centrally located from the standpoint of air power. Over the new transpolar air routes Alaska was no longer isolated, in war or peace, from the world's main population centers.

World War II ended once and for all Alaska's isolation from the nation and shattered the commonly held myths that it was uninhabitable and inaccessible. Some 300,000 men in the armed services saw Alaska for themselves. Many liked what they saw and returned to Alaska after their discharge. Similar was the reaction of many of the tens of thousands of war workers brought into Alaska to build defense installations.

The economic effects of the war in Alaska were enormous. As military bases were rushed to completion and as an endless stream of servicemen and defense workers poured into the territory, the relatively sluggish economy went into a headlong boom.

The Alaska Highway alone was a major factor in quickening the economy and in breaking the territory's long-time transportation bottleneck. Such a highway had long been discussed by the United States and Canadian governments. Pearl Harbor ended the delay. The Army rushed in

seven engineering battalions and 30,000 civilians were hired under fifty-four different contractors. The men worked ten hours a day, seven days a week, under the most adverse conditions. A sign in the hiring hall of one contractor announced: "This is no picnic. . . . Men will have to fight swamps, rivers, ice, and cold. Mosquitoes, flies, and gnats will not only be annoying but will cause bodily harm." But the men signed up and the work proceeded. By the spring of 1944 the highway was completed. It provided the military a valuable supply line to Alaska and at last gave Alaska a land link with the United States. Moreover, it spurred construction of connecting roads which served major cities such as Seward, Anchorage, and Fairbanks.

The war developed large areas of Alaska, and Fairbanks and Anchorage boomed into major cities. Bases, airfields, weather stations had to be built. Harbors had to be dredged. Housing had to be constructed for military and civilian personnel. Federal funds helped communities build water and sewage plants and other facilities.

Another effect of the war was to hasten the integration of Alaska's Indians, Aleuts, and Eskimos, who served valiantly in the armed services. Many of them acquired valuable technical training in service and were able to return to civilian life as air pilots, mechanics, and skilled workers. Old "No Natives Served Here" signs were eliminated during the war, and the legislature passed antidiscrimination legislation. Funds were appropriated to combat the growing tuberculosis rate among the native population.

The war unified all Alaska's people, native and white, and gave them a greater sense of Alaska's importance to the United States. They knew for the first time not only that Alaska was essential to the national welfare but also that it was so considered by a growing number of Americans and certainly by the military establishment in Washington.

After the war was over, Alaska remained a major defense bastion. Although the United States and the Soviet Union had been allies during World War II, relations between the two countries deteriorated when the cold war started in the late 1940s. Alaska's proximity to Russia gave it a new importance.

Ladd Air Force Base near Fairbanks became a center for U.S. fighter-interceptor jet planes. At Eielson Air Base were stationed the heavy bombers of the Strategic Air Command. Fort Richardson and Elmendorf Field, both near Anchorage, became two of Alaska's largest military installations. Here were established headquarters for the Alaskan Command, coordinating all United States forces in Alaska, the Alaskan Air Command, the Army. Navy headquarters were at Kodiak.

Alaska became a center for Army and Air Force experimentation in combat under arctic conditions. Army doctors tried out new drugs to reduce susceptibility to frostbite. Planes were tested in the bitter winter of Alaska's interior, and the use of chemical warfare in extreme cold weather was explored. The development of radar led to the establishment of the DEW Line — distant early warning system — which runs across Canada and Alaska.

Alaskans, separated only by the few miles of the Bering Strait from Russia, continued to hope even during the worst tensions of the cold war era that the United States and the Soviet Union could resume friendly relations. They continued hoping that Alaska could fulfill its destiny as a bridge of peace betwen Europe and Asia. But they knew that in any case Alaska had become an important part of the modern world, whether in war or peace.

15

STATEHOOD AT LAST

ERNEST GRUENING, a short, gnomelike man with a gruff voice and a twinkle in his eyes, saw Alaska for the first time in 1936, when he was forty-nine years old. It was a case of love at first sight. Almost from that moment Gruening's driving purpose in life became to help Alaska achieve its rightful place, to take the great stride forward to statehood.

Gruening's career had been full and varied before he devoted himself to Alaska. He looked like the kind of country doctor who was loved by his patients — and he had, in fact, been trained as a physician. As a young man he became a journalist and writer. He had been the editor of the New York *Post* and several other leading publications and was the author of several authoritative studies of Latin America.

Then under President Franklin D. Roosevelt he entered government service and was appointed director of the Division of Territories and Insular Possessions. One of the territories in his division was of course Alaska. That was how he eventually became interested in the vast northern area. He was delighted when the President named him governor of Alaska in 1939, a position he occupied until 1953.

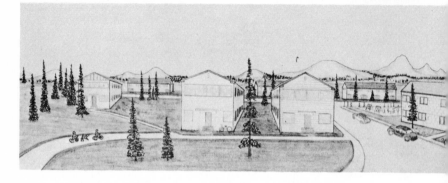

He was thus in a position to lead Alaska during the critical war period and to develop the postwar program which prepared Alaska for statehood.

Gruening acted vigorously to continue the growth begun by the war. Under his leadership, the legislature set up agencies to build Alaska's economy and to promote private and public housing. The legislature not only voted bonuses for veterans but also approved loans up to $10,000 so that they could acquire homes, farms, and businesses.

It seemed to Gruening, as well as to many others, that the early postwar period was the right time to start the big push for statehood. Of course, Alaskans had dreamed about statehood long before. Back in 1916, James Wickersham, then Alaska's delegate to Congress, had introduced the first statehood bill. But in those days statehood was just a dream. There was too much opposition both in Congress and within Alaska itself. It was World War II that first made statehood a practical possibility by developing the territory's economic resources and by ending Alaska's isolation from the rest of the nation.

In the struggle for statehood that started after the war, Gruening was the master strategist and the guiding genius. One Alaska government official put it this way: Wickersham was Alaska's lead-off batter; Gruening was the clean-up batter who won the game in the last inning.

Actually, the drive for statehood began before the war was over. In December 1943, only a few months after Attu and Kiska were recaptured, Alaska's delegate to Congress, Anthony Dimond, introduced a statehood bill. He had little hope for immediate action. But he wanted to pose the issue — and a real issue it had at last become.

Delegate Edward Lewis Bartlett, Dimond's successor who later became one of Alaska's first United States senators, introduced a new statehood bill in 1945. The Alaska territorial legislature for the first time that year voted overwhelmingly to urge Congress to admit Alaska as the forty-ninth state, and in 1946 the legislature conducted a referendum of the state's voters which showed a majority of better than 60 per cent for statehood. A significant minority still felt, however, that Alaska was not ready for statehood, and there were also fears that statehood would mean higher taxes.

When Bartlett again put in his bill in 1947, it began to be taken seriously. For the first time in Alaska's history, formal hearings on a statehood bill were held before a congressional committee. Scores of Alaskans, elected officials, business people, ordinary citizens, spoke eloquently for statehood. And on their side now were high public officials. From General of the Air Force H. H. Arnold came this plea for statehood:

In this world of tomorrow, Alaska is assured a position of great importance. Upon Alaska our future may well rest. What, then, would be better; what would insure a greater provision for our future than to recognize that most important area and make it a state, equal to our forty-eight states?

Secretary of the Interior Julius A. Krug argued for statehood in a statement which summed up the long grievances of Alaskans against coutrol of its government and its economy by absentee interests:

Alaska has suffered for many years under what is virtually a colonial system that has encouraged absentee exploitation of its natural resources without leaving enough social and economic benefits for the territory. If Alaska is granted statehood, its people will have more to say about their economic as well as their political destiny. Absentee interests, working for their special ends, will find it more difficult to dominate the economy of the area. This type of financial control will continue just as long as the Alaskan people find it necessary to travel six thousand miles to Washington in order to obtain the legislative action which they need to deal with their problems.

During the next few years, Alaskan statehood became an almost constant issue in Congress. Bills were introduced; hearings were held: congressional committees made repeated trips to the territory to examine its resources and its readiness for statehood. More and more congressmen came to the conclusion that statehood was not such a wild and visionary scheme after all. Both Democratic and Republican national conventions endorsed statehood. So did organizations of every kind — labor, farm, veterans, and women's.

Within Alaska, too, sentiment for statehood was becoming almost universal. A Senate committee reported in 1951 that there was little opposition to statehood in Alaska and that "the burden was carried by representatives of the fish-packing industry with headquarters in the states."

Despite this massive support, statehood bills got nowhere in Congress for more than a decade. The Bartlett bill which had gotten off to such a promising start in 1947 was pigeonholed. In 1950 the House passed statehood bills for both Alaska and Hawaii, but the Senate killed the measures. In 1952 statehood lost in the Senate by only one vote. In 1954 the Senate finally voted to approve statehood for Alaska and Hawaii — but the House failed to act.

What was holding up statehood?

The arguments against Alaska were old and shopworn. One senator kept insisting that Alaska's climate was so terrible that "brief exposure means instant death." Another maintained that Alaska was too barren to sustain a substantial population.

But speeches of this kind were no longer as persuasive as they had once been. Many members of Congress had visited Alaska and were familiar with the facts.

Senator Magnuson of Washington bluntly told his colleagues that one of the behind-the-scenes forces blocking statehood was the power of the Alaska fish-canning industry with headquarters in his home town of Seattle. The possibility of higher taxes and of loss of political influence resulting from statehood apparently troubled the canning industry and other interests with investments in Alaska.

But the most serious obstacle was partisan politics. Statehood became a political football, kicked back and forth by the House and the Senate, by the Democrats and the Republicans. Statehood for our two remaining territories, Alaska and Hawaii, was linked in Congress. Republicans feared that Alaska would elect Democrats to Congress. Democrats feared that Hawaii would elect Republicans.

Besides, influential southern senators threw their strength into the balance against statehood. Dedicated to the cause of white supremacy, they assumed, and accurately so, that both Alaska and Hawaii would elect senators and representatives who would support civil-rights legislation to aid racial minorities and that this would weaken the southern bloc in Congress.

There was a deadlock in Congress, and somebody had to do something to break it. Alaska decided at this point to move full steam ahead for statehood. In 1955 the legislature showed its confidence in statehood by calling a constitutional convention which drafted a modern, streamlined constitution for what it confidently expected would become the forty-ninth state. Submitted to the voters in 1956, it was ratified by better than a two-to-one vote.

Alaska also pushed statehood with what has been called the Tennessee plan. In 1796 Tennessee had prodded a reluctant Congress by electing two senators and sending them on horseback to Washington in advance of the formal approval of statehood. A number of other territories subsequently followed that example, and so did Alaska. In 1956 Alaska elected two senators and a representative and sent them to Washington to lobby for statehood. Their effective work was backed up by *Operation Statehood,* an organization which raised funds and issued printed material supporting the cause.

By 1957 the pressure for Alaska statehood became almost irresistible. Both Senate and House committees approved statehood bills. The measure was stalled in the House Rules Committee for almost a year. But time was running out for the opposition.

To speed the inevitable, Alaskans made two compromises. They agreed to a provision postponing state control of their fisheries and wildlife until the Secretary of the Interior certified that they were able to manage these resources "in the national interest." They also went along with a provision giving the President power to withdraw almost half of Alaska from administration by the state in the event of national emergency. On the other hand, the statehood bill not only granted all the rights of self-government but also provided for turning over to the state more than 100 million acres of federally owned land.

The final act in the statehood drama was fast-moving. The House voted for statehood on May 28, 1958, by a vote of 208 to 166. There was some grumbling when the bill came up in the Senate. A few Senators regaled their colleagues with horror stories about Alaskan weather. "The climate, which cannot be changed by legislation, is a distressingly forbidding feature of this vast area," said one. But the Senate voted 64 to 20 for statehood on June 30. The rest was formality. President Eisenhower signed the bill July 7. In August Alaskans ratified the congressional action by better than a five-to-one vote.

Alaskans knew after the Senate vote that statehood was at last a reality — and the night of June 30, 1958, will long be remembered in the forty-ninth state. It was warm all over Alaska, and in the north it was a night of the midnight sun. Men and women, dressed in summer clothing, danced in the streets. They didn't know their state had just been described on the Senate floor as uninhabitable, and in view of the vote that followed they didn't much care. That night bonfires burned in celebration, guns boomed, flags were unfurled, and sirens sounded.

When the rejoicing was over, Alaskans faced up to the big job ahead. They now had to substitute orderly, democratic government for the inherited chaos of the past. They were reasonably well prepared to cope with their new problems. Alaska had planned ahead: a streamlined state constitution ready to go into operation. In the fight for statehood Alaska had developed capable leaders and a democratic participation in public affairs which now proved invaluable.

Appropriately enough, Ernest Gruening, longtime veteran of the fight for statehood, was elected United States senator from Alaska in the state's first election. Elected senator along with Gruening was Edward Lewis Bartlett, Alaska's delegate to Congress for many years. Ralph J. Rivers, Alaska's first member of the House of Representatives, was a former mayor of Fairbanks and a former attorney general of the territory. Rivers and Gruening had both been in Washington as members of Alaska's Tennessee-plan delegation to lobby for statehood.

Alaska's first elected governor, William A. Egan, former airplane pilot, cannery worker, truck driver, and grocer, had played a leading and constructive role in the constitutional convention three years earlier, and most members of the state legislature, as well as the appointed officials, had valuable experience in government.

The new state government promptly reorganized the more than one hundred overlapping territorial boards, commissions, and departments into twelve streamlined departments. Alaskans set up a state system of courts, and new judges dived into a backlog of three thousand cases which had piled up in Alaska's overworked federal courts.

There had been no territorial courts or prisons before, and the whole judicial system was in chaos.

The new state government faced the overriding task of promoting Alaska's economic growth and stability. Alaska's economy after World War II had been sustained largely by defense expenditures. It is estimated that as much as two billion dollars has been spent on defense installations in Alaska during and since the war. Alaskans welcomed the improvements and the jobs created by military construction. But they sought new industries to balance the economy and to offset the decline of Alaska's traditional mainstays, gold mining and salmon fishing and canning. Economic expansion was needed to provide jobs for Alaska's growing population, which had reached 210,000 by the time of statehood.

From the very outset, statehood helped improve Alaska's economic situation. Statehood eliminated the Jones Act, which for almost thirty years had increased the cost of living and of doing business in Alaska by artificially hiking transportation rates. As a state, Alaska no longer had to beg for its share of appropriations for federal programs. It was now entitled as a matter of right to appropriations on the same basis as all other states for schools, roads, airways, and public-works construction. In addition, the federal government provided about twenty-four million dollars to help tide Alaska over the transition to statehood.

By January 1960 Alaska was permitted to take control of its fisheries and thus stop the use of fish traps and other destructive practices which had disastrously cut down the salmon pack. The state was also planning to make available to businessmen and citizens the vast acreage which it would receive from the federal government over a twenty-five-year period.

Statehood for the first time brought democracy to Alaska and made it possible for Alaskans to be represented in Congress, to govern themselves, to have a voice in determining their own destinies. It gave them at last the opportunity they had so longed for, to develop and build the great, rich land mass of Alaska.

16

A LONG VIEW

WHAT will Alaska be like in 1980? Will Alaska's pioneers win their battle to conquer the forces of nature, to wrest the treasures of the great land from its mountains and rivers and people its broad expanses with flourishing, prosperous communities?

Or will they go down to defeat, thwarted by natural obstacles and the indifference of their fellow citizens?

Engineers, economists, and other experts give optimistic answers to the questions. They are convinced that Alaska will become more than ever the land of opportunity, providing employment and fulfillment to the young and energetic; that its population will be at least a million and a half, more than six times its present size; that its landscape will blossom with great cities and mighty industries.

They believe that Alaska will be both workshop and playground, providing a vacation retreat for all North America and perhaps much of the rest of the world; that millions of people will fly in every year for a few days or a few weeks to find in its vast spaces an escape from the overcrowding and the strains of modern life.

They see the distinct possibility that man will succeed in

moderating the rigorous climate in some areas of Alaska, that crops will have a longer summer in which to grow, that man-made projects will make even barren soil fertile.

Jet planes will fly into Anchorage and Fairbanks in five hours or less from New York and Washington, with Tokyo and elsewhere in the Far East another similar hop. Alaska's long isolation from the rest of the United States and from Europe and Asia is already over. Alaska in 1980 will be the hub of busy air traffic from all over the world. An Alaska vacation for hunting or fishing will be no more ambitious than a trip to Miami or to California.

This isn't fantasy. It is already a simple matter for tourists to fly to Alaska not only from the West Coast but from other parts of the United States as well. In 1960 there were direct flights to Anchorage from New York and Minneapolis.

Airlines of other countries have discovered that the northern great circle route is the short cut between Europe and the Far East. The legendary Northwest Passage has been found at last — through the air. DC–7 airliners now make the flight to Anchorage from Paris in seventeen hours and take another fourteen to Tokyo. Jets, now being instituted by the main airlines, cut the flying time drastically.

Planes will probably be hopping back and forth across the Bering Strait between Siberia and Alaska twenty years hence, and Nome may well become a major air terminal for travel and commerce between the United States and Russia. A tunnel or a bridge across the strait, long a dream both of Russian and American engineers, could also become a reality. These possibilities depend not on new and miraculous feats but on the ability of America and Russia to live at peace and to settle their differences at the conference table.

Imagine a streamlined, luxurious Arctic Express pulling into Fairbanks daily after a fast railroad trip from Chicago via Canada. A direct railroad connection with the rest of the United States has been another longtime dream of Alaskans — and even this is becoming increasingly practical. A study of the feasibility of such a route was begun in 1960 by the United States–Canadian International Railroad and Highway Commission.

Comfortable train travel will, of course, give visitors an alternate and extremely scenic route to Alaska. With improved air and railroad facilities will also come new motor roads linking isolated southeast Alaska with the interior, and Nome on the Being Sea with the rest of the state.

But probably the biggest effect of new railroads and highways will be to eliminate at last the transportation bottleneck which has so long retarded the development of Alaska's natural resources. They will make it possible for Alaska to unlock the treasures hidden in its forests and mountains and to supply the entire world with raw materials.

This isn't a fantasy either. It has also just begun to come true. Late in 1960 a sleek Japanese freighter anchored in Sitka's harbor while longshoremen filled its hold with processed wood pulp to supply Japan's synthetic textile and plastic factories with raw materials — dresses and suits for the Orient from Alaska's limitless forests.

For twenty-five years former Governor B. Frank Heintzleman, a longtime forestry expert, crusaded for the utilization of Alaska's timber. He argued that with proper conservation practices the new state's great forests could provide lumber and pulp to the United States and other countries for generations. Now at last this dream, too, is being realized. A giant pulp mill has been in operation in Ketchikan since 1954; another huge mill at Sitka, financed by Japanese funds, went into operation in 1960. And there are other plans now under way to utilize Alaska's forest resources.

Japanese geologists have been looking over Alaska's vast unused coal deposits with a view to obtaining coal to produce coke for Japan's factories. It would save the Japanese time and money to bring in coal from Alaska instead of the East Coast of the United States. Alaska has vast quantities of coal, iron ore, and copper which can help supply the world's mounting demand for minerals and which will be mined and shipped economically as soon as production costs can be reduced by improved transportation and cheaper sources of fuel.

Will Alaska in 1980 be in the midst of a new gold rush — a scramble for the black gold called oil? Will oil wells and refineries dot the mountains and tundras of the forty-ninth state? Will Alaska oil millionaires be as numerous as those from Texas?

Oil prospectors have already been hard at work in Alaska, and their forecasts are optimistic. These prospectors haven't traveled on horseback or by dogsled over dangerous mountain passes. They have been traveling by helicopter, using modern instruments in their search for the geological formations that indicate oil. Ground crews following up the helicopter prospectors found a rich oil well on the Kenai Peninsula near Anchorage in 1957. Several oil and natural gas fields have been discovered, and in 1960 some forty companies were engaged in exploration.

An oil boom in Alaska, if it actually takes place, will revolutionize the state. Oil production on a large scale will require pipelines, refineries, roads, and a myriad of supporting industries. Gas and oil prices will come down. Truck and auto transportation will become much less expensive than they have been. If natural gas fields are brought into production, they will provide cheap fuel for a modernized, industrialized Alaska.

What about atomic energy? Here is another potential source of power and fuel for a growing Alaska. Scientists have long favored the use of atomic power plants in underdeveloped areas. Atomic energy, supplementing the use of coal, oil, and natural gas, may help Alaska's new industries. The Army has contructed a six-million-dollar nuclear power plant for its own use at Fort Greely in the interior. Successful operation may pave the way for construction of similar plants at a cost low enough to bring inexpensive electricity and power everywhere in Alaska.

There is another plan for providing Alaska with cheap electric power: harnessing the energy of its great rivers. One proposed project at Rampart Canyon on the Yukon, about a hundred miles northwest of Fairbanks, would provide twice as much power as any hydroelectric plant functioning anywhere in the world in 1960.

A dam at Rampart Canyon, part of the planned power development, would also soften the climate of Alaska's interior and provide new opportunities for its farmers. This dam would back up the Yukon for 150 miles. The result would be a 7500-square-mile lake, an artificial inland sea which would warm the climate of the interior and lengthen the growing season in that area by at least six frost-free days. It would stimulate development of a new and important agricultural area, providing water for irrigation and cheap electricity for farmers.

The most radical proposal so far for changing Alaska's climate and turning the entire state into a temperate productive area has come from Peter M. Borisov, a Russian engineer highly regarded by his government. Borisov believes that the ice sheet of the Arctic can be melted by building a fifty-five-mile collapsible dam on reinforced concrete pontoons across the Bering Strait. Powerful pumps would suck cold water from the Arctic Ocean into the Pacific. This, he claims, would permit the Gulf Stream, which flows from the Atlantic into the Arctic, to melt the northern ice pack. The Arctic Ocean would then become a great natural heating plant by absorbing the sun's rays while ice and snow reflect them into space.

Carrying out such a plan is far in the future, and action to change the weather would have to be preceded by a change in political climate. It would require human engineering as well as great scientific skill. The United States and the Soviet Union would have to cooperate closely to make any such vast climate-changing project possible. Besides, competent American engineers have grave fears that this project might backfire and ultimately produce a new ice age over much of the earth's surface.

Even without drastic, far-reaching schemes of this sort, modern science and technology have the know-how now to transform Alaska, to develop its water power, to utilize its oil, its minerals, its forest, to make its soil fertile and productive, to build up a transportation system linking it with the entire world. Other regions with climate similar to Alaska's — the Scandinavian countries and Siberia, for example — have been developed to a considerably greater degree. Surely the United States can do at least as much in its northernmost state.

It will not be easy to make up for the long years of neglect, and it will not be done overnight. Alaska needs sustained growth rather than another get-rich-quick Klondike. The job cannot be done by speculators and promoters or by men anxious to get what they can out of Alaska and return home in a hurry. It will be done by hard-working engineers, scientists, technicians, teachers, skilled laborers, businessmen, professionals.

Modern pioneers of this type are even now engaged in taming our last frontier and laying the basis for the future growth of Alaska. As a result of their efforts, the Alaska of tomorrow will emerge as a populous, prosperous state. Thousands of engineers will plan and operate the industries built on the basis of Alaska's unlimited resources. Great new cities, with every electronic convenience, will spring up in what are now empty prairies and forests.

In the new Alaska just beginning to emerge, there will be opportunity and hope for the young people of the new state and for thousands of others from all over the country. Students, now wrestling with the mysteries of mathematics and science, will have their chance in Alaska to build a thriving, modern civilization in areas that are now wilderness, to make use of the resources of our richest state for the benefit of the nation — and of the world.

The flourishing Alaska of 1980 is a dream and a promise — one that young people now growing up can help make real.

APPENDIX

SOME DATES IN ALASKA HISTORY

1741	Alaska discovered by Alexei Chirikov and Vitus Bering, explorers in the service of the imperial Russian government.
1784	First permanent settlement by Russians in Alaska, on Kodiak Island.
1799	Russian-American Company formed to conduct fur trade and to rule Alaska; Alexander Baranof named as manager and governor.
1802	Baranof founds Sitka, establishing a fort there.
1804	Sitka recaptured by the Russians from the Tlingit Indians and made the capital of Alaska.
1867	Secretary of State William H. Seward buys Alaska from Russia for $7.2 million.
1867–84	Period of no civil rule or government in Alaska.
1884	Alaska given a civil government under the Department of the Interior.
1880	Gold found in southeast Alaska.
1896	Gold discovered in the Canadian Yukon near Alaska.
1897	The great Klondike gold rush starts.
1898	Gold found in Nome on the Bering Sea.
1900	Laws strengthening civil government in Alaska are passed.
1906	Juneau becomes the capital of Alaska; Alaska allowed to elect a delegate to Congress; Alaska's coal lands closed to private interests.
1912	Alaska made a territory and permitted to elect a legislature.
1916	First Alaska statehood bill introduced in Congress by James Wickersham.
1923	Government-owned railroad between Seward and Fairbanks completed.
1935	Matanuska Valley farming colony started.
1942	Invasion of the Aleutian Islands by Japan.

167

1944   Japanese ousted from Attu and Kiska islands; Alaska Highway, linking the United States, Canada, and Alaska completed.

1947   First congressional hearings on Alaska statehood.

1956   State constitution adopted in Alaska and final push for statehood launched.

1957   Successful oil well brought in on Kenai Peninsula.

June 30, 1958   Alaska statehood approved by Congress.

January 3, 1959 Alaska proclaimed a state by President Eisenhower.

SOME FACTS ABOUT ALASKA

Area: 586,400 square miles — one fifth the size of all the other states combined. Alaska is 900 miles from north to south, 2700 from its eastern boundary to the western tip of the Aleutian Islands — farther than from New York to San Francisco.

Mountains: Alaska has three principal mountain ranges: the Pacific Range, along the south and southeast coastline; the Alaska Range in central Alaska, which merges with the Aleutian range to the southwest; the Brooks Range, which runs from east to west across northern Alaska above the Arctic Circle. Tallest mountain in North America is Mount McKinley, 20,320 feet, part of the Alaska range.

Rivers: The Yukon and its tributaries, the Porcupine, Tanana, and Koyukuk rivers, compose one of the great river systems of North America and drain all of central Alaska. The Yukon rises in British Columbia, is more than 2000 miles long and runs along the entire breadth of Alaska, emptying into the Bering Sea.

Population: Alaska's population in the 1960 census was 225,000. It is estimated that this includes 16,000 Eskimos, 14,000 Indians, and 4000 Aleuts. Population has risen rapidly in the last twenty years: it was 72,524 in 1939 and 128,653 in 1950.

SOME ALASKA TERMS AND EXPRESSIONS

ALCAN. The name originally applied to the Alaska Highway, still used by many Alaska residents. A combination of the names Alaska and Canada.

AURORA BOREALIS. Northern lights seen in arctic skies, usually in early evening. Supposedly explained by electrical discharges in upper atmosphere.

BAIDARKA (plural BAIDARKI). Single- or double-hatch hunting boats made of skin by the Aleuts.

BARBARA. Aleutian hut, made of sod and driftwood.

BANANA BELT. Term applied to southeast Alaska, suggesting that some Alaskans consider this area the tropics of the North.

BELUGA. The ten-foot white whale used by the Eskimos as a major item of food.

CHEECHAKO. Newcomer, tenderfoot.

HOOTCHENOO. Powerful Indian home brew, origin of the American slang expression *hootch*.

IGLOO. An Eskimo dwelling of sod and timber — not iceblocks.

ICE WORM. Refers to an old Alaska joke started by a gold-rush newspaperman who made up a story about the worms that came to the surface of the ice on a cold night. The story was taken seriously all over the world, and Alaskans made the most of it. Bartenders used to put strands of spaghetti in drinks and tell tourists they were ice worms. More recently, real ice worms — tiny black creatures — have been discovered.

KAYAK. Small Eskimo boat made of skin, with an opening at the top just large enough for one man.

MALEMUTE. Sled dog.

MUKLUK. Eskimo fur boot.

MUKTUK. An Eskimo delicacy, the outer skin of the whale with a layer of fat attached, eaten raw.

MUSH. *Move!* An Indian version of the French *marche*.

NELUKATAKTUT. The Eskimo blanket-tossing game, played with a walrus hide.

OOGRUK. A large variety of seal, used by Eskimos for food and clothing.

170

OUTSIDE. The rest of the United States. An Alaskan taking a trip to Seattle, for example, says he is going "outside." Despite statehood, the term is still frequently used.

PARKA. A warm Eskimo jacket, usually made of fur. Pronounced "parky" in Alaska.

PERMAFROST. Permanently frozen ground water, beneath the top layer of soil which thaws in spring.

POTLACH. The feast of southeast Indians, marked by days of eating and then by gifts of many prized possessions from the host to his guests.

POKE. A sealskin bag used for storing blubber; also refers to the hide bags used by sourdoughs for gold dust and thus to "roll" or wealth.

PROMYSHLENNIKI. Russian frontiersmen and hunters who came to Alaska from Siberia.

SIWASH. A contemptuous term for Indian or native, from the French *sauvage*.

SKOOKUM. An Indian word for big, strong.

SOURDOUGH. An old-timer in Alaska, a name that came from the fermented dough used by the prospectors who didn't have yeast. Sourdough pancakes are still Alaska favorites.

SQUAW CANDY. Pieces of hard, dry smoked salmon, considered a delicacy by the Indians.

TUNDRA. The swampy, rolling plains that cover much of the interior and the arctic areas of Alaska.

UMIAK. A large Eskimo skin boat.

WILLIWAW. Sudden, changing winds which blow up off the Alaska Peninsula and the Aleutian Islands.

SOME BOOKS ON ALASKA

For those who would like to do further reading on Alaska, this brief list is culled from the thousands of available books on the subject.

FICTION AND POETRY

BEACH, REX. *The Spoilers*. New York: Harper, 1907. Story of the hectic days in Nome when claim-jumpers conspired to steal valuable gold mines.

————. *The Iron Trail*. New York: Harper, 1913. Rival interests clash over the route of Alaska's first railroad.

————. *The Silver Horde*. New York: Harper, 1909. The bitter battle between prospectors and the salmon cannery interests.

FERBER, EDNA. *The Ice Palace*. New York: Doubleday, 1958. Interesting fictionalized account of Alaska's struggle for equality and statehood.

LONDON, JACK. *The Sea Wolf*. New York: Macmillan, 1904; reissued 1937. Adventure in the Bering Sea.

————. *Burning Daylight*. New York: Macmillan, 1910; reissued in 1934. About the gold rush days in the Yukon. A prospector who strikes it rich decides he doesn't want his wealth after all.

————. *The Call of the Wild*. New York: Macmillan, 1903; reissued in illustrated edition 1956. Story of a superb dog and his devotion to his master in the wilds of the Yukon.

————. *White Fang*. New York: Macmillan, 1906; reissued 1935. Another good story about a dog in the Yukon and how he is finally tamed.

SERVICE, ROBERT. *The Spell of the Yukon*. New York: Dodd, Mead, 1939. Ballads of the gold rush, including "The Shooting of Dan McGrew" and "The Cremation of Sam McGee."

HISTORY

BERTON, PIERRE. *Klondike Fever*. New York: Knopf, 1959. History of the gold rush to the Yukon by a Canadian newspaperman and historian.

172

CHEVIGNY, HECTOR. *Lord of Alaska.* New York: Viking, 1942. Dramatic biography of Alexander Baranof, the man who built the Russian empire in America.

COE, DOUGLAS. *Road to Alaska.* New York: Messner, 1953. The epic story of the Alaska Highway.

GRUENING, ERNEST. *The State of Alaska.* New York: Random House, 1954. The authoritative and standard history of Alaska under United States rule and of the long fight against discrimination of various kinds.

TOMPKINS, STUART. *Alaska.* Norman: University of Oklahoma, 1945. The Russian period is emphasized in this general history of Alaska.

REMINISCENCES, ADVENTURE, EXPLORATION

HUBBARD, BERNARD R., S.J. *Mush, You Malemutes.* New York: America Press, 1932. The glacier priest tells true stories of adventure in Alaska.

NELSON, KLONDY and COREY FORD. *Daughter of the Gold Rush.* New York: Random House, 1959. Experiences of a young girl during the gold rush days and after.

STEFANSSON, VILHJALMUR. *My Life with the Eskimos.* New York: Macmillan, 1913; reissued 1951. Authentic account by a famed explorer of life in the Arctic, includes much valuable information about the Eskimos.

WICKERSHAM, JAMES. *Old Yukon: Tales, Trails, and Trials.* Washington, D.C.: Washington Law Book Co., 1938. Reminiscences and stories about Alaska in the old days by the man sourdoughs consider the father of statehood.

POTTER, JEAN. *The Flying North.* New York: Macmillan, 1947. The thrilling story of Alaska's pioneer flyers.

NATIVE LORE AND LEGEND

KEITHAHN, EDWARD L., with illustrations by GEORGE AHGUPUK. *Alaska Igloo Tales.* Seattle: Seal, 1958. Authentic Eskimo tales with drawings by an outstanding Eskimo artist.

BARBEAU, MARIUS. *Alaska Beckons.* Caldwell: Caxton, 1947. Indian myths and folklore told and explained by an expert in the field.

MCCORKLE, RUTH, with illustrations by WILBUR WALLUK. *Alaskan*

Ten Footed Bear. Seattle: Seal, 1958. Native legends for readers of all ages.

NATURE AND WILDLIFE

CARRIGHER, SALLY. *Moonlight at Midday*. New York. Knopf, 1958. Beautifully descriptive of Alaska wildlife and scenery.

GABRIELSON, IRA N. and FREDERICK C. LINCOLN. *Birds of Alaska*. Harrisburg: Stackpole, 1958. A must for the bird lover. Illustrated information on 321 species of birds encountered in Alaska.

GENERAL

ADAMS, BEN. *Alaska: The Big Land*. New York: Hill & Wang, 1959. An over-all view of Alaska's geography, history, spots of interest for visitors, economics. Illustrated with 150 photographs.

BUTLER, EVELYN I. and GEORGE DALE. *Alaska: The Land and the People*. New York: Viking, 1957. An intimate account of Eskimo and Indian life written especially for teenagers by two long-time educators in Alaska.

Guide to Alaska and the Yukon. Box 856, Cathedral City, Calif. Helpful information for tourists.

HILSCHER, HERB and MIRIAM. *Alaska, U.S.A.* Boston: Little, Brown, 1959. Two Alaskans tell about the challenge and the rewards of life in Alaska today.

Mid-Century Alaska, Washington, D.C.: Government Printing Office, 1957. A handbook of information compiled by the Department of the Interior.

INDEX

INDEX

177

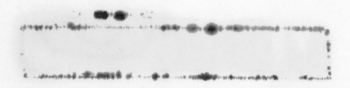